Community out of Partnership

Community out of Partnership: The Evolving Story of the Learning Representatives of the Educational Institute of Scotland

Alex Alexandrou

humming earth

Published by

Humming Earth
an imprint of
Zeticula
57 St Vincent Crescent
Glasgow
G3 8NQ
Scotland.

http://www.hummingearth.com
admin@hummingearth.com

ISBN-13	978-1-84622-027-0	Hardback
ISBN-10	1-84622-027-0	Hardback
ISBN-13	978-1-84622-028-9	Paperback
ISBN-10	1-84622-028-9	Paperback

Dedicated to the memory of

Tony van der Kuyl (1946-2008)
and
Niki Valanidou (1989-2008)

Contents

Preface

This book is dedicated to the memory of two people who were tragically and prematurely taken from us. Tony van der Kuyl was a colleague and friend from the University of Edinburgh and International Professional Development Association and Niki Valanidou was the young daughter of my cousin Elenitsa. Although one passed away in Scotland and the other in Cyprus, they had one key thing in common. They were both passionate about education with Tony making an incredible contribution to education developments in Scotland and on the international stage whilst Niki was loving every minute of her time at university.

They are sadly missed but their passion for education is shared by a unique group of people that I have had the pleasure and privilege of working with for a number of years. They are the Educational Institute of Scotland's (EIS) Learning Representatives (LRs) who on a voluntary basis advise and guide their colleagues in respect of their lifelong learning and professional development ambitions. By helping their colleagues and promoting the professional development agenda in Scottish education, they are ensuring that future generations of Scottish children will benefit from the improved practice of their teachers.

This is my second book charting the development of the EIS teacher LRs based on a study I carried out between 2007 and 2008. It examines the second main cohort of local authority based teacher LRs and the first main cohort of school based teacher LRs.

The book aims to give the reader a detailed account of the professional development agenda within the compulsory sector in Scottish education from both a policy and practitioner perspective leading to a unique insight into how this group of volunteer lay representatives are helping to shape the professional development agenda at both the strategic and operational level, in a way that was not envisaged during their inception in the early part of this century.

Acknowledgements

This volume would not have been possible if it was not for the support and participation of a number of individuals and organisations and I am taking this opportunity to show my appreciation of their involvement.

Firstly, I would like to thank the Scottish Government for funding that ensured that a study took place leading to this book.

Secondly, I would like to thank the Educational Institute of Scotland's (EIS) Learning Representatives and National Officials; representatives from the Scottish Government, General Teaching Council of Scotland (GTCS), National CPD Advisory Group, Her Majesty's Inspectorate for Education (HMIE), Local Authority Continuing Professional Development Quality Improvement Officers (LA CPD QIOs) and Directors of Education, the University of the West of Scotland (UWS) and the teachers and head teacher who gave of their valuable time to be interviewed and surveyed.

I would like to mention in particular the significant assistance I have received from Lyn McClintock, the EIS Learning Representatives Administrator, Simon Macaulay, EIS Assistant Secretary, Veronica Rankin, EIS National Officer (Education and Equalities), Eleanor McConchie, EIS Administrative Assistant (Union Learning Department) and all my colleagues at the University of Edinburgh, particularly Dr Jim O'Brien, Dean of the School of Education. As always their guidance and facilitation have proved invaluable in ensuring the study has progressed smoothly and that I have been able to access all available individuals and sources required.

Finally, but not least, thanks to Clare and Louie for their love, patience and support.

Alex Alexandrou
Edinburgh
May 2009

Introduction

Context

In Scotland, both the present Scottish Government and previous Scottish Executive have put a great deal of emphasis on the continuing professional development (CPD) of educators. For school teachers, this has come in the form of the *McCrone Report* (2000) and the subsequent *21st Century Agreement* (Scottish Executive Education Department (SEED), 2001). In addition, the Scottish Government (2007) has published its key strategy for lifelong learning and professional development entitled *Skills for Scotland*. These initiatives have given the lifelong learning and professional development of teachers and the role of LRs greater impetus within the Scottish teaching profession. Particularly, as commentators such as Clough (2008) and Moore and Ross (2008) have highlighted the growing emergence and evolvement of union learning representatives (ULRs) within the UK.

Aims of the Book

This book, which is the second in a series charting the evolving EIS LRs initiative aims to examine the creation of a CPD community made up of teachers, LRs, head teachers and local authority CPD Quality Improvement Officers (QIOs), and the impact it is having on the compulsory sector. It will highlight and discuss the formation of this community and how the ensuing partnership approach is working at different levels within Scottish teaching. As Hollinrake et al. (2008: 392) state the '...role of trade union learning representatives (ULRs) and the broader union learning agenda have become an increasing focus of academic debate' and this book hopes to add to this body of work from the unique perspective of the Scottish education sector.

Research Approach

This study is underpinned by the Democratic Evaluation approach to educational research, where the voice of the participant is primary (Alexandrou, 2007; House, 1993; Kushner and Norris, 2007 and Stake, 2005). To back this up and ensure greater validity a mixed methods approach was adopted as Ivankova et al. (2008:3) state:

'Mixed methods research is characterized by collecting, analysing and "mixing" both quantitative and qualitative datasets at some stage of the research process within a single study to understand a research problem more completely...Mixed methods research with its focus on the meaningful integration of both quantitative and qualitative data, provides the breadth and depth that a single approach, either quantitative or qualitative, lacks by itself...It requires understanding of multiple contexts, establishing a trustworthy relationship between researcher and participants, and addressing concerns of diverse participant groups'.

The data for this study has been collected using a number of approaches. Firstly, background information was collected using recently published policy documents and academic literature. Secondly, EIS national officials and other Scottish education stakeholders were either interviewed personally, by e-mail or by telephone or wrote a personal record. This was in order to give me as the researcher greater context, practice-based views and observations as to the current situation and their relationship with the EIS LRs. Thirdly, teachers and one head teacher were either interviewed personally or answered a short questionnaire survey. Fourthly, the second cohort of LRs (36 in total) were asked to participate in the study by completing a questionnaire (in some cases two distinct questionnaires); writing a personal record of their experiences to date and participating in consultation forums and question and answer sessions at their regular LR meetings. Fifthly, I attended and observed a number of CPD events organised by LRs and LA CPD QIOs.

The interviews were based on a semi-structured approach and participants were free to answer as many or as few of the questions that were put to them. They also had the opportunity to determine where and how the interview took place. The majority of the interviews were face-to-face in either the participants' working environment or hotels. One interview was conducted by e-mail and another by telephone due to time constraints in both cases.

This study in the main focuses on the second group of 36 LRs. Unlike the first study, this group of LRs is a mix between authority-based (more commonly referred to as Multi-Establishment (ME)) and School-based LRs. There are thirteen ME-based LRs and twenty three School-based LRs in this cohort.

In terms of the questionnaire, the participants were asked to give demographic details; why they chose to become a LR; their relationship with their institutions, school management, LA CPD QIOs and local associations; experiences in dealing with colleagues; CPD initiatives they have been involved in and time-off and funded cover arrangements. The participants were also given the opportunity at the end of the questionnaire to make further comments on any of these or other issues.

As the study progressed and more jointly organised (between LRs and LA CPD QIOs) CPD events were held, a number of the LRs involved in them were approached to complete a questionnaire about the events and their experiences. The participants were asked how the idea of a joint CPD event came about: their working relationship with LA CPD QIOs; outcomes of the event for them as LRs; if their profile had been raised amongst colleagues and if there were plans for future joint events. The LRs were also given an opportunity to make further comments on any of these or other issues if they so wished.

In relation to the personal records, the participants were asked to volunteer to write them and informed that not all of them were expected to participate in this phase of the evaluation. They were asked to consider a number of issues (some of which had been dealt with in the questionnaire) and as a guide I produced a list of issues to help them structure the focus of their responses. Participants were also encouraged to write on any issue they felt was important.

In order to build upon the data collected from the questionnaire, and to ensure that the voice of the participants clearly came through in the process, writing a personal record was considered the best approach. As with more time on their side, participants would be able to deliberate for longer and deeper about the issues surrounding their roles as LRs, which would not necessarily be the case if they were interviewed.

In addition to the questionnaire and personal records, the LRs at their quarterly meetings participated in question and answer sessions and ad-hoc consultation groups with me. This method allowed me to update continually my knowledge of how the LRs were progressing and what issues they were facing at the time.

This data was supplemented by a short questionnaire survey of teachers conducted face-to-face at a CPD event. The survey asked the participants if they were members of the EIS; read the Institute's journal on a regular basis; knew what a LR was and had utilised the services of a LR. I also attended and observed a number of CPD events. I carried out these additional stages of the study in order to investigate further issues highlighted by the LRs and the other stakeholders who had been interviewed. Kushner (2000) describes this approach as interrogating the data with data.

In total, thirty six questionnaires were distributed and thirty two were returned, which meant there was an overall response rate of 88.9%. Breaking these figures down further, twelve out of the thirteen ME LRs returned their questionnaires, which equated to a 92.3% response rate, whilst twenty out of twenty three School LRs returned theirs, equating to a 87% response rate. Six of the LRs filled in the CPD events questionnaire and seven of the participants agreed to write a personal record. Thirty teachers (who were varied in terms of position and length of experience) were approached at a CPD event to participate in a short questionnaire survey and all of them agreed to participate.

The following were all personally interviewed: the National CPD Co-ordinator; GTCS's CPD Professional Officer; an Assistant Chief Inspector of HMIE; six LA CPD QIOs; four teachers; one head teacher and the UWS's Co-ordinator of the EIS LR undergraduate and post-graduate training modules. Additionally, one Director of Education and one EIS National Officer submitted either a personal record or statement.

Such a significant response to the main phase of the evaluation from a variety of stakeholders in a relatively short time-frame indicates that this cohort of LRs and the other participants are committed to the concepts of LRs and teacher CPD and had faith in the evaluation process, which in turn helps to validate the data and findings.

In all cases and in keeping with the British Educational Research Association's revised ethical guidelines (BERA, 2004) informed consent was sought and gained with all the participants and where requested by certain respondents (and promised by the evaluator), identities have been concealed to protect them.

The aim of this approach is not only to ensure the validity of the research process but also to triangulate the data. As Creamer (2008: 3) points out 'Triangulation is associated with using multiple sources of data to confirm findings', thus ensuring the findings, concluding thoughts and observations stand up to scrutiny.

The Structure of the Book

Chapter 2 outlines how the key stakeholders in Scottish education are monitoring the progress of teacher professional development. It will concentrate on major reports by Audit Scotland and Her Majesty's Inspectorate of Education that have examined the progress to date of the *21st Century Agreement* and the Scottish Government initiated review of the Chartered Teacher (CT) Project. These initiatives will be examined from not only a practitioner perspective but also linked into the current academic debate surrounding CPD and CT.

Chapter 3 will highlight the Scottish Government's lifelong learning and skills agenda concentrating on its key strategy document entitled *Skills for Scotland: A Lifelong Strategy*. This strategy not only promotes the concept of partnership working amongst stakeholders it also lays down specific challenges to individuals, employers and trade unions in terms of their commitment and what is expected of them in relation to the lifelong learning and skills agenda for Scotland. It clearly shows that the Scottish education system has a key role to play in ensuring that it works and the role that EIS LRs will need to play to ensure that this is the case.

Chapter 4 begins to assess what has been achieved since the first study by highlighting developments from both an internal and external perspective. It outlines the initiatives the EIS has undertaken and by examining the view of key stakeholders that represent the GTCS, HMIE, National CPD Advisory Group and Aberdeenshire Council.

Chapter 5 begins to analyse the primary data in relation to the LRs in-depth concentrating on the demographic profile of the LRs and why they took on the role. The analysis is aided by the insights of Karen Gilmore of the UWS, who is the Co-ordinator of the EIS LRs training modules and Lyn McClintock, the EIS LRs Administrator.

Chapter 6 examines how the LRs are being supported by stakeholders at local level with the aim of highlighting to what extent they have become accepted and embedded within EIS local associations and local authority and school CPD structures. It will discuss the extent to which they have been integrated into their local association structure; their experiences of being accepted by headteachers and the time-off and funded cover arrangements in place for them to carry out their role and responsibilities.

Chapter 7 addresses the challenge set by the Scottish Government for stakeholders to work in partnership to promote and implement its lifelong learning and skills agenda. It does this by examining how the EIS LRs are working together with both their Local Authority CPD QIOS and School CPD Co-ordinators to develop and improve their working relationship, with particular emphasis on the CPD QIOs. It will highlight how this has been achieved by describing in some detail the organisation and delivery of joint CPD events and how the LRs are slowly but surely being co-opted onto CPD related working groups and committees with some positive outcomes

Chapter 8 seeks to examine whether the positive working relationship built up between the LRs and their CPD counterparts at local authority and school level is having an impact on their colleagues in terms of being able to connect with them. It will analyse the degree to which significant numbers of teachers seek advice and guidance from them and the types of interaction they have with colleagues. This is achieved by not only seeking the views of the LRs but also Karen Gilmore, Lyn McClintock and teachers themselves through detailed one-to-one interviews and a questionnaire survey.

Chapter 9 examines the impact the role has had on this cohort of LRs. It highlights additional obstacles and problems the LRs have encountered; the LRs views on their role; the effect it has had on them form a personal and professional perspective and how in their view their role and responsibilities can be developed.

Chapter 10 brings the book together by highlighting the key issues and themes that have emerged from the analysis. It then offers a number of observations the strategic and operational stakeholders within the Scottish education system can draw upon to further strengthen the LRs initiative by advocating further capacity building be undertaken to ensure the long-term sustainability of the EIS LRs.

The book concludes with a short postscript on developments since the study was completed.

2

The Professional Development Agenda for Scottish Teachers

Introduction

The *McCrone Report* (2000) and *21st Century Agreement* (SEED, 2001) have ensured that CPD for Scottish teachers is a key element of the Scottish Government's education strategy in terms of raising the professional aspirations of teachers and helping to improve the quality of teaching delivered in Scottish schools.

This chapter will detail how the strategic stakeholders are monitoring CPD developments. It will begin by dealing with recent reports by Audit Scotland (2006) and Her Majesty's Inspectorate of Education (2007a) that have examined the progress of the *21st Century Agreement* (SEED, 2001) concentrating on the CPD and Chartered Teacher (CT) elements of these reports as they are the most pertinent to this study.

Audit Scotland's and HMIE's Initial View of the 21st Century Agreement

In May 2006, Audit Scotland published a report that examined the implementation of the *21st Century Agreement* (SEED, 2001) based on questions such as:

- What measurable outputs have been achieved with the funding provided?
- Have the milestones for change contained in the Agreement been met?
- Have the changes brought about by the Agreement made teaching a more attractive career? (Audit Scotland, 2006: 3).

The report stated that: '…The study does not assess the impact of the Agreement on the quality of teaching and educational attainment of children' (Audit Scotland, 2006:3).

The HMIE's report in relation to the progress of the *21st Century Agreement* (SEED, 2001) followed in January 2007. It highlighted the importance of the quality of teaching required and the importance of CPD if the aims and objectives of the agreement are to be achieved. The inspectorate's stance was laid out very early on in the report when it stated that if:

> '…Scotland's children are to succeed educationally, socially and economically we need to deliver an education system which is not only of the highest quality to meet the learning needs of today but which is flexible and responsive enough to equip our children with an education which will serve them well in an uncertain future. Of critical importance to learning is the quality of teaching and the professional skills, attitudes and attributes that successful teachers bring to the learning process' (HMIE, 2007a: 3).

This is a direct and powerful statement and indicates that CPD and CT are crucial elements if the above are to be achieved. This implies that there will be a key role for EIS LRs to play and the more colleagues they assist through effective advice and guidance, the more likely it will be that a greater proportion of teachers will take up CPD and CT opportunities, thus, helping to impact positively on and improve teachers' classroom practice.

The Audit Scotland report stated that virtually all the milestones set for 2004 had been met bar one and it found that there had been '…increased and more consistent access to CPD opportunities for teachers' (Audit Scotland, 2006: 9). As for the CT scheme the report explained that:

> '…Although the Scottish Executive set no specific target figure for numbers likely to participate in the scheme, the numbers of teachers currently participating in the scheme (2,800) and who have successfully completed the scheme to date have been small. These numbers are lower than the Scottish Executive's financial modelling would have suggested (based on the costs associated with the salary enhancements which accrue to teachers upon completion of the scheme). Only 45 per cent of the estimated amount required was used in 2004/5' (Audit Scotland, 2006: 14).

In relation to CT, the HMIE highlighted similar issues to those raised by the Audit Scotland Report, particularly in relation to the expectations and uptake of CT. It observed that:

'Initially, some education authorities had set high expectations (25-30%) for the proportion of non-promoted staff who would enter and move up the six points of the chartered teacher scale. However, uptake of the chartered teacher programme was significantly lower than these figures in all authorities…This meant that the ability of chartered teachers to make a positive impact on the learning and teaching in schools was as yet limited' (HMIE, 2007a: 8-9).

Audit Scotland and the inspectorate are correct in highlighting the uptake figures which they point out are low. However, it is important to note that the CT scheme is relatively new and it will take time for teachers to embrace the CT concept. As the first evaluation highlighted there is still deep cynicism amongst teachers in relation to CPD and CT. This is backed up by Connelly and McMahon's (2007) recent survey of teachers following the CT programme. When asked what their colleagues thought about them undertaking the CT programme the teachers stated they had encountered hostility and negativity. Connelly and McMahon (2007: 101) point out such reactions hinted at:

'…CT being a clandestine or isolating activity, whereby teachers choose not to reveal to colleagues that they are pursuing it. As a consequence they risk missing out on potential encouragement and support, while the school loses out by not being a partner in teacher development and change'.

This resentment will take time to work itself out of the system of not only individual teachers but also the education sector in general. As Connelly and McMahon (2007: 101) state the hostility '…may subside with time as CT becomes an accepted part of the CPD framework'.

The evidence suggests EIS LRs will have a crucial role to play if there is to be a sustained uptake of CT and the HMIE (2007a:9) is encouraged that 2,000 teachers are now on various points of the CT scale. Connelly and McMahon's (2007: 101-102) findings add weight to the inspectorate's optimism that teachers are embarking upon the CT programme due to the following reasons: professional development; financial motivations; fulfilment of the need for intellectual stimulation; improving personal status and recognition; disinterest in a management route to enhancement and that they have a significant '... desire to engage in formal processes for developing personally and professionally'.

The inspectorate also noted that:

> 'In addition to the low numbers of teachers joining the scheme, another weakness was that teachers were able to self select for the programme. Headteachers and education authorities had no opportunity to influence the selection process and were therefore unable to ensure that the best teachers were participating' (HMIE, 2007a:9).

This observation indicates that EIS LRs and LA CPD QIOs working together can do more to encourage uptake of CT and help teachers make the correct decisions in terms of their professional development be it through CT or other routes. It can be argued that EIS LRs are in a good position based on their training, knowledge and expertise to advise colleagues as to their suitability for CT. They are trusted colleagues who have no economic or political axe to grind. Matthew MacIver, (formerly Chief Executive of the GTCS) is of the opinion that the EIS LRs should not only be the first port of call for their colleagues in relation to CPD and CT but also are the people who can be most trusted by teachers (Alexandrou, 2006: 15).

As highlighted in the first study and alluded to above, the teaching profession is sceptical of the CT scheme and the HMIE clearly found this to be the case as the following observation shows:

> 'Many teachers did not regard the chartered teacher programme as an attractive proposition. The reasons given included money and time costs for individual teachers. Few teachers appeared to accept the argument that the cost of qualifying through the stages would be balanced by salary increases as they moved up the scale, or that relatively young teachers could enjoy up to 25 years of enhanced salary once they had reached the top of the chartered teacher scale. Few teachers agreed that the chartered teacher route had the potential to provide fulfilment in their careers' (HMIE, 2007a: 9).

In relation to CT, Audit Scotland made the following observations in terms of the impact of the scheme:

'The new Chartered Teacher Scheme has not yet had the expected impact on the career structure for classroom teachers. [The] Scottish Executive indicated that 30,000 teachers were eligible to participate when the scheme was introduced in 2003 of whom around 6,000 indicated an interest. By February 2006, 2,800 teachers were participating in the scheme and 201 teachers had achieved full chartered teacher status, the vast majority of these by the accreditation route.

Newer entrants to the profession appear much more willing to participate in the scheme than those who have been in the profession longer. Seventy-four per cent of those who have been teaching for less than three years say it is likely that they will participate in the scheme in the future, compared with 32 per cent of classroom teachers overall. While it is unlikely that all of these teachers will participate, the positive attitude among newer entrants means that uptake looks set to rise as these teachers become eligible to participate.

The main reasons that classroom teachers are likely to participate in the scheme are to further their career opportunities (39 per cent), further develop their teaching skills (39 per cent) and for the additional salary (38 per cent).

In contrast, teachers who have been in the profession longer are significantly less likely to participate in the scheme in the future. The percentage of those likely to take part in the scheme drops from 40 per cent among those who have been teaching for three to ten years, to 15 per cent among those in the profession between 11-20 years, down to three per cent of those who have been teaching for 21 years or more. The main reasons given by those teachers unlikely to participate are that it is too expensive (31 per cent) and time consuming (24 per cent).

If a future increase in uptake of the scheme is fuelled primarily by newer entrants to the profession, as would seem to be indicated from the evidence, there is a danger of a two-tier system emerging among classroom teachers. There is a need to ensure that high-quality teaching practice continues to be expected, and recognised among all teachers, regardless of chartered teacher status' (Audit Scotland, 2006: 30).

Reeves (2007: 66-72) vividly highlights this problem in her study, as the cohort of CT teachers she evaluated raised a number of issues and problems when undertaking a project linked to their collaborative professional enquiry module. These included: clear problems in undertaking collaborative enquiry with colleagues; teacher culture being a barrier to negotiating access with all colleagues and school managers and there were differences in principle between the process of action enquiry and school development planning.

These observations indicate there is much work to be done in convincing the teaching profession of the merits of CPD and the CT concept. Again it can be argued that the EIS LRs have a crucial role to play in helping to change attitudes as they can be regarded as trusted confidantes who are there for the benefit of colleagues to help them achieve their long-term aspirations.

However, Reeves (2007: 62) in her survey of the CT initiative is very positive about the scheme and argues that

'The clear commitment in this Standard [for Chartered Teacher] to criticality and independence of judgement as a characteristic of teacher excellence in Scotland is both heartening and surprising, given that the Scottish system is as swamped with paper, performance indicators and targets as anywhere else in the UK. What this standard affords for both providers of Chartered Teacher programmes and those teachers who wish to achieve the status is a space in which to assert a form of teacher professionalism which is in marked contradiction to the educational operationalism model'.

In relation to CT, Audit Scotland concludes that the:

'...changes to be brought about by the Agreement were seen by the signatories to it as a long-term process, perhaps spanning a whole generation of teachers and pupils. This means that forming judgements on some aspects, for example, its impact on educational leadership and performance improvements (such as school attainment levels), can only take place once an appropriate period of time has elapsed; certainly longer than the five years which has currently passed since the Agreement was signed.' (Audit Scotland, 2006: 15).

Significantly, in relation to CPD in general, the Audit Scotland report states that the '...*quality and variety of CPD has improved under the Agreement'* (Audit Scotland, 2006: 24) and goes on to highlight that:

'Our evidence indicates that the additional 35-hour maximum CPD has been put in place across Scotland. Of those teachers interviewed in our survey, 93 per cent reported that they have a CPD plan and 96 per cent an individual CPD record'.

Whilst the HMIE (2007a: 19) noted that:

'Almost all education authorities found the introduction of 35 hours of CPD to be relatively straightforward, and had built purposefully on existing staff review and development procedures...[and that almost]...all teachers had now accepted the mandatory nature of the 35 hours of CPD and had taken full responsibility for maintaining their development profile'.

This is an encouraging finding in one sense but the question is are teachers doing just enough to ensure that they tick the box when it comes to completing their 35 hours of CPD to comply with regulations rather than using this opportunity to take advantage of professional development opportunities to improve their practice and job prospects? Again this is another example of where EIS LRs can play a critical role in ensuring that the latter is the case for the reasons cited above.

Audit Scotland reported that:

'The teachers we surveyed are generally positive about the benefits of the additional CPD. Eighty-three per cent feel that CPD increases teacher skills and 75 per cent feel that it improves curriculum development. Only half (51 per cent), however, feel that it improves teacher motivation.

There is a noticeable difference in attitude by length of time in teaching. Those who have been teaching less than three years are markedly more positive towards the new arrangements and the benefits arising from them, than those who have been teaching longer.

While teachers are positive about the benefits of the additional CPD time, it is difficult to assess educational benefits and value for money as few local authorities have put in place effective monitoring and evaluation schemes.

Opportunities exist to learn from other professions where CPD is an integral part of career development (eg, law, medicine, accountancy)' (Audit Scotland, 2006: 24-25).

The HMIE (2007a: 20) backs up Audit Scotland's findings noting that:

'Increasingly, schools were taking a broader view of what constituted CPD. Approaches were often underpinned by the idea that teachers benefited most when training focussed on improving learning and teaching and was attuned to their own classroom practice'.

Whilst:

'Mandatory CPD reviews were now embedded in the practices of all authorities. Most education authorities had implemented a system of yearly reviews...[and] ...Education authorities were increasingly introducing follow-up surveys on the impact of CPD on learning and teaching by asking teachers, six or nine months after they had participated in training to recount how their teaching had improved as a result of the training...However, there was little evidence as yet of sufficiently effective and cohesive monitoring and evaluation of the impact of CPD on pupils' experiences and attainment at school level' (HMIE, 2007a: 20-22).

In relation to CT, the above findings are backed up to a degree by firstly, Kirkwood and Christie (2006: 439-441) who in their limited evaluation of one CT module found their teaching cohort to be very positive about it. They show that:

'...module activities had facilitated interchange of opinions and sharing experiences; the content was stimulating, challenging, and reflected current thinking and research; module activities had enabled respondents to be more creative when planning lessons and teaching, and to apply ideas from research to their own teaching; and the assessment approach was ideal. For some participants, the module had the effect of injecting a feeling of renewed enthusiasm and confidence...

... [There was] further evidence of the positive impact on professional practice, which had continued beyond the duration of the module. There are, for example, accounts of successful attempts to link theory to practice resulting in significant shifts in practice, and of respondents adopting a research perspective on their own teaching...

...A further development indicating the sustainability of their [cohort being evaluated] professional and personal commitment was the involvement of nine former participants within a collaborative learning community in which various forms of enquiry on teaching thinking were pursued'.

Secondly, Connelly and McMahon (2007: 98-100) found that their small cohort of teachers engaged on the CT programme had benefited from it in terms of engaging with new ideas or educational research, developing confidence and that their schools had to some extent benefited from their CT activities as the following quote indicates:

'The fact that a number of respondents were able to identify benefits for their pupils is encouraging and is an indicator of the impact of the practice-related focus of CT courses and assessments'.

Thirdly, Reeves (2007: 64-65) found that by the end of the first module her cohort had completed, positive changes in classroom practice had been noted, notably: the teachers had a greater sense of agency, self-confidence and increase in expertise; had developed an ability to cite texts to justify their actions and opinions; became more confident in trying new things in the classroom and teachers felt the module had also allowed them to reclaim some of their classroom autonomy.

The HMIE (2007a: 22) is also positive about the future of CT and CPD as it concluded that:

'Overall, the Teachers' Agreement has stimulated and supported the development of a more comprehensive and rigorous approach to all aspects of CPD. It has led to staff having access to a wider range of CPD opportunities, supported by education authorities and partnerships with private companies and universities. For many staff, the Teachers' Agreement has led to increased levels of self-awareness and a sense of focus on personal and professional needs. It has helped many to understand the importance of CPD in improving the learning experience and achievement of pupils'.

A positive conclusion and one that can be built upon as EIS LRs in partnership with CPD QIOs work together to encourage more teachers to look upon CPD as a positive experience from both a personal and professional perspective. Particularly, as Audit Scotland recommended that the Scottish Executive (now Scottish Government):

'...in partnership with other parties to the Agreement, needs to identify a comprehensive set of outcome measures against which the ongoing cost and impact of the Agreement can be assessed. Measures could cover areas such as:
- impact on educational attainment
- improvements in classroom practice
- the quality of educational leadership
- workload and skill-mix
- workforce morale
- recruitment and retention within the profession' (Audit Scotland, 2006: 32).

The analysis of the two reports and supporting academic findings indicates that the EIS LRs may well have a key role to play in sustaining and pushing forward the CPD and CT agenda. Significantly, the LRs were not mentioned once in either report unlike the other stakeholders they work with. However, it must be noted that following contact with HMIE personnel in relation to this study and members of the inspectorate reading and discussing the first evaluation, I was notified that HMIE inspectors were hoping to meet EIS LRs in the inspectorate's next set of school visits (Carlisle, 2007).

Review of the Chartered Teacher Project

Following on from the Audit Scotland and HMIE reports, the then Minister for Education, Hugh Henry announced a review of the Chartered Teacher project (SEED, 2007). In its covering letter explaining why the review was taking place SEED (2007) explained that the:

'...background to this review is that while the Executive is committed to rewarding excellence in classroom practice we consider that the time is right to review the impact of the project. In particular we want to consider whether there are any improvements that can be made'.

Some of the key issues that the review considered were: eligibility criteria, age profile of those undertaking the CT project and issues affecting uptake of the Chartered Teacher project (SEED, 2007). The Chartered Teacher Review Group (CTRG) reported in June 2008 and it can be concluded that there is strong support for the CT initiative as the following statement indicates:

'The Group wish to highlight their support for the original principle behind the CT scheme which was stated by the McCrone Committee in their Report...The recommendations in this Review Report are intended to continue to support and further develop the CT scheme in line with the original principle' (CTRG, 2008:8).

This comment should be regarded in a positive light in relation to the CT initiative and could help to embed the EIS LRs further in the CPD and CT communities of practice that are being established within the Scottish teaching sector. Particularly, as the Group found that:

'...in some areas of the scheme [CT] is not actively promoted by either the local authority or school senior management team' and '...there was a considerable amount of anecdotal evidence relating to inconsistent, insufficient and inappropriate deployment of CTs, that some headteachers were unsure as to what they could require of CTs, and that some CTs wanted to do more or less than was being required of them' (CTRG, 2008: 11-13).

As with Audit Scotland and the HMIE, the Group found '... there was a lack of evidence around the impact on and outcomes for learning and teaching of the CT scheme' (CTRG, 2008: 13). In the light of these and other findings the Review Group made a number of recommendations. The recommendations of the Review Group indicate a long-term future for the CT scheme and one can deduce from them that there is a key role for the EIS LRs to play in helping to implement them. For example, the third recommendation which states that '…all stakeholders should actively promote the CT scheme' (CTRG, 2008: 9). However, what is noticeable by its absence is any mention of the EIS LRs and the role they can play in helping to sustain the CT initiative.

The Review Group echoed the findings of Audit Scotland and the HMIE in relation to the relatively low uptake of CT. It stated that as of September 2007 '…we had 521 full CTs and over 2,000 who were working their way through the scheme'. The Review Group went on to highlight that cost, time commitments, career progression and the lack of promotion of the CT scheme in some areas by either the local authority or the school management team (as highlighted above) mitigated against many teachers signing up for CT scheme (CTRG, 2008: 11).

However, it did point out the salary enhancements accrued as a result of achieving CT status was a positive factor in teachers joining the scheme (CTRG, 2008: 11). Connelly and McMahon's (2007: 98) study also found financial motivations as one of the key reasons along with professional development, fulfilment of the need for intellectual stimulation, improving personal status and recognition and a disinterest in a management route to enhancement for embarking on CT.

The observations of both the Group and Connelly and McMahon indicate that EIS LRs can play a key role in promoting CT amongst colleagues and encouraging those who are eligible to sign up. They should also pick up on Reeves (2007: 62) observation that in the CT scheme there is a clear commitment '…to criticality and independence of judgement as a characteristic of teacher excellence in Scotland'.

In her response to the Review Group's report, Fiona Hyslop, the Cabinet Secretary for Education and Lifelong Learning reiterated the Scottish Government's support for CT. The Cabinet Secretary highlighted that as of June 2008, there were 611 accredited CTs with almost 2,500 working through the programme and emphasised that it was crucial '...that we use the skills of Chartered Teachers to the full for the benefit of children and young people' (Hyslop, 2008: 1).

However, the minister expressed '...a degree of frustration and disappointment that they [the Review Group] seem to have ducked some of the most difficult issues' (Hyslop, 2008: 2-3) and highlighted a number of areas where she felt there was the potential to push the scheme forward For example, teachers to consider seeking the endorsement of their school management to participate in the CT scheme; demonstrating to colleagues school-based evidence that needs to be validated; that schools recognise teachers who have achieved CT status as a valuable resource and to fully utilise them and asking the HMIE to '...undertake a review of the impact of Chartered Teachers in Schools. This will give us valuable information about the current position; and it will allow us to identify and disseminate good practice' (Hyslop, 2008: 3-7).

The Cabinet Secretary's observations have implications for all education stakeholders including the LRs. It seems that the EIS LRs could well have a role in advising teachers as to how to include senior colleague endorsement in relation to their suitability for CT and the type of school-based evidence required; advising their CT accredited colleagues in relation to the role they could and should play within their schools and provide evidence to the HMIE (based on their experience of advising and helping colleagues) in relation to the inspectorate's proposed study of the impact of CT in schools.

This chapter has concentrated in the main on the CT initiative but it must be noted that there are a number of other CPD routes that can be pursued. For example, significant emphasis has been placed on and resources allocated to identifying and developing the future cadre of school leaders, through the Scottish Qualification for Headship (SQH). As SEED (2002) stated the SQH '...was introduced to ensure that people who wish to become headteachers can obtain the professional development opportunities they need prior to their appointment'. Cowie and Crawford (2007) and Reeves et al. (2005) have critically assessed the SQH programme in its formative years and along with the Organisation for Economic Co-operation and Development (OECD) (2007) and the HMIE (2007b) highlight the importance and necessity of leadership development within the Scottish education system. Thus, the LRs have a role to play in advising and guiding colleagues in relation to this programme.

The next chapter will highlight the recent policy debate surrounding the lifelong learning and skills agenda as set out by the Scottish Government.

3

Scottish Government's Lifelong Learning and Skills Agenda

Introduction

Since devolution there has been a strong emphasis on improving the knowledge and skills of the Scottish workforce through lifelong learning. The Scottish Executive (as highlighted in the first volume) during Labour's period in office and the Scottish Government led by the Scottish National Party (SNP) have fully embraced this concept through public pronouncements and strategic policy initiatives. Their initiatives have highlighted the importance of working in partnership with other stakeholders, notably trade unions to achieve their aims and objectives in relation to the skills agenda. This is significant as Hoque and Bacon (2008: 702) in their assessment of trade unions, ULRs and employer-provided training in the UK point out that based on the OECD's statistics the '...UK skills base is weak by international standards'.

In turn, this will have a significant bearing on how the EIS LRs will and should operate, as union learning representatives (ULRs) have the support of the key strategic stakeholders within government. For example, the Scottish Executive (2003) with its five-year lifelong learning strategy entitled *Life Through Learning: Learning Through Life* and more recently in support of the Scottish Trades Union Congress' (STUC) workplace learning and ULRs initiatives (STUC, 2007: 5-6).

The Scottish Government's Challenge

The Scottish Government (2007) with its *Skills for Scotland: A Lifelong Strategy* is continuing with the message and the strategy as epitomised by Fiona Hyslop, who states that a:

'...smarter Scotland is at the heart of everything we want to achieve for this country. We can only build a Scotland that is wealthier and fairer, one that is healthier, safer, stronger and greener, if people are equipped with the skills, expertise and knowledge for success...To achieve our vision we need to work with all our key partners' (Scottish Government, 2007: 2).

At the heart of this strategy has to be the education system and teachers will play a key role, hence the importance of their lifelong learning and professional development. This indicates a role for EIS LRs in helping their colleagues with their CPD and in part the Scottish Government achieve its aims and objectives. This is clear from the following statements from the strategy document:

'Young people's education, from the early years of a child's life through their compulsory education, coincides with a period of rapid development and lays the foundations of skills for life and work. What they learn and how they learn have a major bearing on wider outcomes including employability and participation in society in later life...

...In recognising the crucial role played by the early years workforce in skills development, we are introducing requirements that will mean all leaders of early years services will be qualified to SCQF Level 9.

Furthermore, to encourage a professional workforce at all levels, staff will be supported by a new integrated qualification and professional development framework that will help them understand how they can develop their careers' (Scottish Government, 2007: 14-15).

The Scottish Government (2007: 33) clearly recognises the role trade unions can play as it states that:

'Evidence shows that trade unions engage with and raise the aspirations in the workplace that other agencies struggle to reach. We will encourage employers and unions to work together, using local learning agreements, to support the development of individuals in the workplace'

and as the strategy document shows through a case study of Rolls-Royce, ULRs are a key element in achieving this (Scottish Government, 2007: 37). From a teaching perspective, EIS LRs will be the designated agents to ensure this will be the case in the education sector.

The Scottish Government (2007: 45) points out that if its strategy is to succeed then:

'Partnership – between Government, employers, individuals and learning and training providers – is the key to delivering on these priorities and our success depends on a shared vision of what we need to achieve'.

It goes on to challenge employers, individuals and trade unions amongst others to ensure that the agenda it has set out can be delivered upon. In relation to employers it urges them to:

'...Understand how training can benefit their performance and their staff and be aware of the range of training and support that is available to them...

...Be prepared to train individuals to develop the employee they want – and be prepared to invest in that training...

...Encourage and facilitate staff to access available learning opportunities...

...Work together with Trade Unions, using local learning agreements, to support the development of individuals in the workplace' (Scottish Government, 2007: 46).

As Lee and Cassell (2009: 6) highlight in their study that deals with the ULR concept in the UK and New Zealand:

'...employers should facilitate learning for their employees because it brings mutual benefits. That is, a more highly skilled workforce offers rewards and greater satisfaction for employees while providing capacity for organisations to compete more readily in a global knowledge economy'.

In relation to individuals the Government states they should:

'Take an active role in shaping their own lives and managing their own learning and development, contributing to their own skills development as far as they are able...

...When in employment, work with their employer to identify and address their learning and training needs...

...Know what is available to them and where to go for information, advice and guidance support' (Scottish Government, 2007: 46).

As for trade unions they need to:

'...Support the development and position of union learning representatives within their organisations...

...Work in partnership with employers to expand the use of local learning agreements...

...Work collectively with the Scottish Government and key partners to help support the creation of a Scottish Union Academy' (Scottish Government, 2007: 50).

For the teaching profession, in concise terms it means that: the EIS has to ensure that it signs learning partnership agreements akin to the one signed with Aberdeenshire Council (Aberdeenshire Council and EIS, 2005) with the other 31 local authorities; local authorities need to ensure that EIS LRs have the required time-off, facilities and funded cover to carry out their role and responsibilities; EIS LRs (both ME and School-based) work in partnership with Local Authority CPD QIOs and School CPD Co-ordinators to enhance the personal and professional development of teachers; EIS LRs actively engage with their colleagues and teachers need to seek out the LRs, LA CPD QIOs and School CPD Co-ordinators to advance themselves.

The following chapters will analyse the primary data to determine to what extent rhetoric is becoming reality.

4

Developing the Learning Representatives Agenda

Introduction

There have been significant developments since the first volume and this chapter will begin to highlight them, particularly where there have been positive changes and also where more work is required. Since the last study the EIS has undertaken the following:

• Initiated an internal debate in relation to constitutional change at local and national level to incorporate the LRs formally within its structures.

• Decided that there is a need for continuing the training and development of the LRs and that not only will a training needs analysis be undertaken but it will also approach a number of professional trainers to help it in this process.

• Developed a strategy with the GTCS to work in partnership.

• Contacted Local Authority Directors of Education and senior CPD personnel to raise the profile of the LRs.

• Engaged in regular consultation with other stakeholders such as the Scottish Government School Directorate (SGSD), HMIE, Learning and Teaching Scotland (LTS) and local authorities.

• Made considerable progress in relation to the time-off issue but is prepared to consider legal action in certain cases if all other avenues have been exhausted.

• Organised a series of CPD seminars for teachers highlighting the benefits of CT and CPD and drawing attention to the role of LRs. The first of these was held in South Lanarkshire in May 2006.

• Actively encouraged its local associations to negotiate learning agreements similar to that signed between the Institute and Aberdeenshire Council.

• Set up a LRs Working Group with a remit to discuss how LRs should give advice and guidance on CPD issues that are not CT related.

- Liaised with the UWS to ensure that relevant changes are made to the LRs training course based on student feedback and discussions with the Institute.

A number of these initiatives will be revisited in the following chapters. Where appropriate the results of this study will be briefly compared with the first study to show where progress has been made and highlight issues and problems yet to be resolved. To begin with the views of a number of stakeholders in the Scottish education system who work with the LRs at the operational level will be highlighted.

The View of Education Stakeholders

In response to both the first and second studies, Bruce Robertson, the Director of Education for Aberdeenshire Council highlighted the importance and significance of the Partnership Agreement the Council has with the EIS as follows:

'I was pleased to note in the evaluation of the EIS's first cohort of Learning Representatives, published in June 2006 Aberdeenshire Council's Partnership Learning Agreement, was regarded as "a model of best practice".

Aberdeenshire Education, Learning & Leisure Service and the Trade Union Learning Representatives have continued to work closely together to ensure that their joint commitments to lifelong learning and CPD are maintained.

Recent developments have included the setting up of Chartered Teacher Networks where meetings are jointly chaired by the authority CPD Support Officer and the Learning Representatives.

The Partnership Learning Agreement (Aberdeenshire Council and EIS, 2005) has undoubtedly developed strong working relationships, which has enhanced the support for teachers in our establishments' (Robertson, 2007).

Margaret Alcorn, the National CPD Co-ordinator, Douglas Cairns, HMIE Assistant Chief Inspector (working in Directorate 5 of the Inspectorate), and Rosa Murray, a Professional Officer of the GTCS, were interviewed for this study. At the time of being interviewed, Douglas had been leading the HMIE team that had gathered evidence for the inspectorate's mid-term review of the progress of the *21ˢᵗ Century* Agreement (as outlined in Chapter 2) of which he was lead author. His answers are based on the findings of the report (Cairns, 2007) and what follows are the observations of all three on the EIS LRs initiative.

The participants were asked when they became aware of the EIS LRs. Margaret first became aware of the EIS LRs in her previous role as CPD Co-ordinator in Edinburgh in around 2001, whilst Rosa who came from a school had not heard of them until she took up her present post in 2004 (Alcorn, 2007, Murray, 2007). Douglas stated that in all four years of compiling the evidence of the report there was not one overt reference to the LRs that he could recollect. The report itself does not mention the LRs (Cairns, 2007). These answers are significant from the perspective that although there is support for the LRs initiative from the key stakeholders, coverage and knowledge of their existence varies from stakeholder to stakeholder and from individual to individual within these stakeholder organisations.

All three were asked what they understood to be the role of LRs and they gave the following answers:

'They are there to advise and guide colleagues on learning in relation to professional development and help colleagues gain access to professional development opportunities' (Alcorn, 2007).

'To advise teachers in their schools about professional development opportunities' (Murray, 2007).

'…is about the CPD of his/her colleagues and about facilitating and co-ordinating CPD for his/her colleagues' (Cairns, 2007).

They were then asked what their initial contact with LRs had been. Douglas stated that he had no contact with LRs but both Margaret and Rosa indicated that they have been in contact with EIS LRs. They have both spoken at national EIS LRs meetings as well as having individual contact with LRs (Alcorn, 2007, Murray, 2007).

Margaret stated it was through Simon Macaulay (EIS Assistant Secretary), CPD initiatives, meetings, general enquiries and access to the EIS. Also in her role, she undertakes visits to local authorities and in this part of her job she has met a few LRs. Her conversations with them give her a feel of what they do. She has also discussed LRs through the CPD Co-ordinators network and how the LRs initiative is working within local authorities (Alcorn, 2007).

Rosa stated that her first contact was through Lyn McClintock (EIS LRs Administrator) by helping Lyn with an in-service session at local level in South Lanarkshire and that '...*it was a great event*'. It worked extremely well and Rosa spoke about professional development. Rosa went on to state that she has done a lot of work in Glasgow but at first she found it difficult to get into Glasgow schools to talk about professional development. However, she overcame this problem with the help of two of the Glasgow-based LRs who fixed up meetings which she could speak at. In turn, Rosa is now organising CPD meetings in Glasgow and the Glasgow LRs have reciprocated by speaking at these events. Rosa has also spoken at two other CPD events organised by EIS LRs in Dumfries and Galloway and Perth and Kinross both of which were a success and well run (Murray, 2007).

Rosa stated that she hopes that EIS LRs who attend her talks on CPD will then away her presentation and use it as they wish when giving talks in schools. This would mean that the GTCS through the LRs will be able to reach many more teachers in Scotland (Murray, 2007).

In relation to the impact the LRs are having Douglas felt that based on the evidence gathered for the report they have not had a lot of impact (Cairns, 2007). Rosa felt it was very mixed and that: the LRs could be building a healthy professional development network; should be giving all teachers and not just EIS members advice and guidance and that it was '...*a jump out of the water for the EIS to create the LRs*'. She went on to state that the LRs she has been involved with are doing great work but it is early days (Murray, 2007).

Rosa highlighted that the amount of professional development opportunities available and the current emphasis on CPD potentially lacks strategy and coherence for a teacher. She felt that if the EIS LRs have the knowledge they could bring the strategy and coherence required. Rosa pointed out that a teacher undertaking professional development does not want to attend a number of isolated courses but wants to construct a coherent picture of their CPD requirements and in her view the EIS LRs could help with advice on this matter (Murray, 2007).

In relation to how the LRs are assisting the three stakeholders in promoting the benefits and understanding of CPD for teachers, the respondents gave mixed answers. Margaret stated that she has tried to engage with the LRs at the two national EIS LRs meetings she has attended in terms of common thinking on CPD (Alcorn, 2007). Rosa pointed out the LRs she and her colleagues have talked to are using the GTCS through the CPD events, where both Rosa and her colleague Tom Hamilton have spoken (Murray, 2007). However, Douglas paints a less positive picture based on the evidence given by teachers to the HMIE on its school visits. He pointed out that nearly 60 schools were visited and the LRs were not of assistance and his negative answer was telling evidence in relation to the profile of the LRs (Cairns, 2007).

When asked how LRs can help improve teachers' understanding of CPD and the benefits of CPD all three respondents highlighted the significant potential the LRs can have in this area to make a positive impact. Margaret stated that it was her core belief that the more capacity the Education sector has and the more people who can help to add value in terms of professional development and reflection, all the better. She felt that LRs will not only be adding value to it but also building capacity (Alcorn, 2007).

Rosa stated that it is the EIS LRs who can advise and guide teachers through all professional development opportunities and help teachers construct a more logical CPD route for themselves (Murray, 2007). Whilst Douglas was of the opinion that there is a big potential role for a person such as a LR who could act as a co-ordinator/facilitator; guide, advise and support colleagues as well as having a leadership role in helping colleagues make informed CPD choices, he also felt that LRs may well have a peer support role and in turn could complement the line management CPD role in schools (Cairns, 2007).

In relation to working with LRs in the future, the stakeholders were positive in their responses. Margaret stated that whilst she had no particular plans in relation to the LRs she is willing and open to engage with them in any form of initiative. She went on to state that she and her team have an inclusive approach and will work with anyone interested in the area of CPD (Alcorn, 2007). Rosa stated that it would be beneficial to build on what has gone on before and to speak or be invited to talk at the national LRs meetings (Murray, 2007).

Based on their observations, the stakeholders were asked how the role of the LRs will and/or should develop in the future. Margaret stated that the LRs are one part of the CPD advice/guidance package and that they should not be seen as the '...*only road to salvation*'. She went on to state that coaching and mentoring were important to her team and she could see the potential for LRs to be involved in that. In turn, this would mean there is a development issue for the LRs to consider. Margaret felt that coaching and mentoring is a potential way forward with the LRs undertaking this to help teachers with their professional development. She went on to point out that a critical mass of LRs has not been reached and the '...*tipping point*' in terms of numbers and the impact of LRs has yet to be reached (Alcorn, 2007).

Rosa was of the opinion that the EIS requires more LRs and there is a need for either a LR in each school or cluster of schools. There should be easy access to them and they should have continuing training after passing the UWS course. Additionally, the LRs should be able to create a community of inquiry/learning within their school or cluster (Murray, 2007).

However, Douglas highlighted a potential problem in terms of conflicting CPD advice and guidance for teachers. For example, there is often a CPD Co-ordinator in each school who may have a management role (as highlighted by Robinson et al., 2008); the teacher's line manager has a role in carrying out a CPD interview with the teacher and then there is the LR. There could be a negative impact in that contradictory advice could be given by a LR, the CPD Co-ordinator and line manager to the same teacher (Cairns, 2007).

Douglas was also of the opinion that the introduction and development of LRs had the potential to refresh the notion that the EIS is a professional association genuinely interested in the professional development of teachers (Cairns, 2007).

In terms of raising the profile of the LRs, the stakeholders made a number of observations and suggestions. Margaret stated that in her opinion there was as yet an insufficient evidence-base in relation to the LRs impact and it still early days in terms of good-practice examples and exciting stories (Alcorn, 2007). Rosa highlighted that their profile needs to be raised and there is a need for local authority partnerships, thus development work needs to be undertaken at this level. She went on to point out that the LRs need to develop partnerships with local authorities and higher education institutions (HEIs) to present, promote and participate in CPD opportunities. For example, setting up CPD events where all stakeholders give a presentation. Thus, the LRs can build up partnerships with local stakeholders and in the future these events can run themselves without Rosa and her colleagues having to turn up and present in person (Murray, 2007).

Douglas believes that LRs could play a greater role and that their role is developing. For example, they could lead for their members in running workshops and having one-to-one impact in schools and ME LRs could have a key role in co-ordinating these types of activities. He also thought it would be appropriate in some circumstances for LRs to sit and work with other colleagues on local authority CPD committees (Cairns, 2007).

Margaret was of the opinion that it was important the LRs see themselves as part of the '...*patchwork of support and development*' in relation to guiding and supporting teachers' professional development. She went on to point out that: all the stakeholders need to keep the doors of communication open; there was a need to keep communicating with each other and it is all about delivering a high quality service in relation to CPD for Scottish teachers (Alcorn, 2007). Rosa felt that the EIS LRs are a great idea and they have put themselves at the heart of teacher professional development. She thinks this has given the EIS a greater educational profile in relation to professional development (Murray, 2007).

The evidence of the operational stakeholders highlights the need for the LRs, firstly, to work in partnership with all individuals and organisations mandated to help teachers with their professional development with the desired impact of helping to raise the profile of and participation in CPD by teachers. Secondly, to raise their profile amongst colleagues and continue to develop their role, for example, by taking on coaching, mentoring and facilitation roles.

The next chapter will deal with the demographic profile and motivations of the second cohort of EIS LRs.

5

The Profile and Motivations of the Learning Representatives

Introduction

Thirty six questionnaires were distributed; thirteen to ME LRs and twenty three to School LRs. In total thirty two questionnaires were returned, which meant that there was an 88.9% response rate. Breaking these figures down further, twelve out of the thirteen ME LRs returned their questionnaires, which equated to a 92.3% response rate, whilst twenty out of twenty three School LRs returned theirs, which meant there was an 87% response rate.

Demographic Profile of the Learning Representatives

Of the ME LRs, seven (58.3%) were women and five (41.7%) were men. For the School LRs fifteen (75%) were women and five were men (25%). As with the previous study these figures to a great degree represent the gender balance of the EIS' total membership which at the end of 2007 stood at 60,121, of which 45,756 (76.1%) were women and 14,365 (23.9%) were men (EIS, 2007). It is worthy of note that in this cohort proportionately more female than male teachers volunteered to become LRs. These figures are particularly striking in two respects, firstly in relation to the School LRs and secondly compared to the previous cohort, more women and fewer men are volunteering to become LRs.

It was noted in the early phase of study that the issue of gender could have had a bearing on how LRs do or do not connect, firstly, with operational stakeholders such as LA CPD QIOs, School CPD Co-ordinators and head teachers and, secondly, with colleagues in terms of their representative role. However, no evidence came to light to suggest that gender was an issue

In terms of age there were significant differences between ME and School LRs. In relation to the ME LRs the results showed three-quarters of this ME cohort were aged between 45-64 years of age, which roughly corresponds to the figures from the previous evaluation; a quarter were aged 25-34 and not one of the ME LRs was under the age of 25, over the age of 64 or aged or aged between 35-44.

However, the age profile of the School LRs differed as proportionately more School LRs were younger than their ME LR colleagues. Not one of the School LRs was aged under 25 or over the age of 64; two (10%) were aged 25-34; seven (35%) were aged 35-44, whilst six (30%) were aged 45-54 and a quarter were aged 55-64.

The participants were asked how long they had been a teacher and as with previous answers there was a variation in answers between the ME and School LRs. In relation to the ME LRs the overwhelming majority (75%) had been a teacher for fifteen or more years, whilst a quarter had 6-9 years service.

The service record of the School LRs differed slightly to the ME LRs. Not one of the School LRs had served less than five years; a quarter had served 6-9 years, another quarter had served 10-15 years and half had served fifteen or more years.

In terms of the sectors the participants worked in there were differences between the two sets of LRs. In relation to the ME LRs, seven (58.3%) worked in the secondary sector whilst a quarter worked in the primary sector and two (16.6%) worked in other sectors, notably Peripatetic SFL P1 – S2 and Specialist Service to Primary and Secondary. However, one of the participants who stated that they worked in the primary sector added that they were on secondment from their school to ICT support covering all sectors. Thus, the second cohort of ME LRs is quite thin on the ground in relation to the primary sector.

As for the School LRs the majority, twelve (60%) worked in the primary sector; six (30%) worked in the secondary sector and two (10%) worked in the special needs sector.

The participants were asked how long they had been employed by their current organisation and the responses showed that a significant majority from both sets of LRs had worked for their institution for ten or more years. However, there was a spread of length of service amongst both sets of LRs.

In relation to the ME LRs, only one (8.3%) had been with their school for two or less years; two (16.6%) had been with theirs for

3-5 years; one (8.3%) for 6-9 years; a quarter had been with their school for 10-15 years and five (41.7%) had been working for their organisation for fifteen or more years.

As for the School LRs: two (10%) had been with their school for less than a year; one (5%) had been with their school for 1-2 years; two (10%) had been with their schools for 3-5 years; a quarter for 6-9 years; a quarter for 10-15 years (with one of these currently on secondment) and another quarter having been with their organisation for fifteen or more years.

The participants were asked how long they had been a member of the Institute and as with the previous evaluation, longevity was a significant factor. Of the ME LRs, not one of the participants had been a member for two years or less; only one (8.3%) had been a member for 3-5 years; a quarter for 6-9 years; just one for 10-15 years and the majority, seven (58.3%) for fifteen or more years.

As for the School LRs, not one of the participants had been a member for less than two years; two (10%) had been a member for 3-5 years; a fifth for 6-9 years, whilst six (30%) had been members for 10-15 years and eight (40%) for fifteen or more years.

Choosing to Become a Learning Representative

The participants were asked if they had held any type of trade union representative post before they had volunteered to become a LR. The responses make for interesting reading and there is a significant divergence between the two sets of LRs. In relation to the ME LRs, eight (66.7%) stated that they had held some type of position before, whilst four (33.3%) had not held any type of position at all prior to volunteering to become a LR. The LRs who stated that they had held positions outlined them as follows:

'Very briefly on [Local Association] *Executive before L Rep (Continuing on the Executive)...LA Secretary: 4 Years...Local Committee of Management for 6 years. Vice-President of the Local Association – 3 years...School/Branch Rep, L.A. Equalities, L.A. Treasurer, EIS Job-Sizing Co-ordinator...School Rep (4y), LA Chair (2y) CAC Rep (4y), Secondary Sector Secretary (2y), Council Member (1y)..I was EIS Rep in 3 schools for about a year each time...School Rep, LA Treasurer...School EIS Representative'.*

The evidence indicates that two-thirds of this cohort of ME

LRs are experienced representatives who "know the ropes" when it comes to representative duties which should stand them in good stead in relation to their LR role and responsibilities.

The picture for School LRs is significantly different. Only six (30%) of the LRs stated that they had held some type of position before, whilst a significant majority, 14 (70%) had not held any position at all prior to volunteering to become a LR. The LRs who stated that they had held positions outlined them as follows:

'School EIS Rep – 7 years…School EIS Representative…EIS Rep for my establishment…School Rep – EIS…Union Rep – 10 years…EIS Rep for school for 1 yr. Health + Safety rep for school for 3 yrs'.

The above evidence indicates that a third of School LRs who have or still are representatives are very much individual school-based representatives with significant experience, which should stand them in good stead for their current role.

Karen Gilmore of the UWS is the Co-ordinator of the EIS LR undergraduate and post-graduate training modules. Karen was interviewed as she and the university play a key role in ensuring that the EIS LRs are equipped to carry out their role and responsibilities. Karen has observed that past and present student LRs who have held or hold other union representative posts are more willing to go in and "fight the corner" as to what the CPD requirements are with their school management compared to those who have not held a position before. The latter are uncomfortable with this approach as they feel they do not have a negotiating role (Gilmore, 2007).

These findings as with the first study raised a number of questions, some that would be answered by other questions in the questionnaires and some that would be pursued in the other stages of the research. The key question at this early juncture was why did members that had held no type of position before become interested in the LR role? Particularly as a significant number of them had not only long service as a teacher but had also been members of the EIS for a considerable time.

In the questionnaires, the respondents were offered a range of options to state why and could choose from more than one option. In relation to the ME LRs they answered as follows:

• Seven stated it was for their own professional development;

- Five stated it was for their own personal development;
- Eight stated it was to improve the professional development of their teaching colleagues;
- Two stated it was because they wanted to become more involved in the EIS;
- Two were inspired by the activities of other EIS LRs and four gave other answers as follows:

'Nobody else would do it!'

'I held back for some time to allow a.n. other to put his/her name forward. None was forthcoming and the job is too important for there to be no Authority/Multi Estab. L-Rep'.

'Lyn McClintock persuaded me'.

'On secondment I enjoy visiting other schools with a wide variety of staff in a supportive role. I've undertaken and now "deliver" a lot of CPD. So the role of LR fits in with the sort of thing I like doing – while potentially being very worthwhile'

As with the responses to previous questions there was a slight difference in emphasis amongst the School LRs as the following answers show:

- Seventeen stated it was for their own professional development;
- Seven stated it was for their own personal development;
- Fifteen stated that it was to improve the professional development of their teaching colleagues;
- Three stated it was because they wanted to become more involved in the EIS;
- None were inspired by the activities of other EIS LRs and three gave other answers as follows:

'Having embarked on the Chartered Teacher modules, I became interested in the CPD opportunities available and all of the above [questionnaire choices] *apply. Also my school at the time (I am now on secondment) was very unfair when deciding the "granting" of CPD courses'.*

'To influence the school management views on teachers' CPD – this is linked to the statement in the 3rd box above [in relation to improving the professional development of teaching colleagues]*'.*

'Being a Chartered Teacher & Mentoring NQTS I became interested in CPD as an area of education'.

The evidence from the personal records back up the findings above and if nothing else show the commitment and enthusiasm this second cohort of LRs have to their role as the explanations below will indicate. One of the ME LR respondents describes why he volunteered as follows:

'My reasons for volunteering to become a Learning Representative were on reflection two fold: I would be able to help others [and] *I would be able to help myself.*

The year I volunteered to become an LR I was also elected to EIS Council and it seemed a logical step to combine the two roles' (Personal Record 1).

This LR went on to state that during the 1980s and early1990s he had been a EIS local representative and significantly this had a positive impact on him in relation to taking on the LR role as he explains below:

'I had a lot of good memories from that era and thought that being a learning rep may have a similar effect on my enthusiasm and that proved to be very accurate. My enthusiasm has definitely improved since I started the LR course' (Personal Record 1).

A School LR gave the following reasons:

'... To consolidate knowledge of the rationale behind CPD and ensure EIS colleagues are achieving entitlement;

To help and enhance my role as school CPD Coordinator, providing information and skills which would be useful to colleagues;

To "give something back" for the CPD opportunities which had been provided to me in the past, by encouraging, mentoring and coaching others' (Personal Record 2).

This School LR is taking her commitment to the cause one step further as she has volunteered to become a ME LR. Another School LR explained why he volunteered as and is a good example of an experienced local representative taking their commitment and passion for looking after the interests of EIS members one step further:

'As a member of the EIS Local Executive, I was made aware of the opportunity to become a School based Learning Representative. With some school staff already (2005) embarking on Chartered Teacher modules and others sifting through the very comprehensive SBC CPD directory, I saw the possibility of being able to assist them with their

options and choices' (Personal Record 3).

The following ME LR displays the passion that many of her colleagues show with this following explanation which takes volunteering to be a LR a step further:

'Equality and Lifelong agendas implicit in a "Teaching Profession for the 21ˢᵗ Century".

The development of a "learning society", one which covers all types of skills and qualifications, and ranging across social, class or social status, age or gender can only be achieved when individuals become actively engaged...

...The personal drivers to commit to the rigours of becoming an accredited LR were those which would give me the credibility to support and mentor co-professionals' (Personal Record 4).

The following explanation by another ME LR takes volunteering for this role even further. It highlights how experiencing the benefits of both CPD and CT first hand can have a positive effect on an individual to such a degree that they are enthused enough to take on the LR role, with no political motive in mind unlike other types of union representative both within the EIS and outwith in other unions:

'I first heard about Learning Reps when I was doing the Chartered Teacher module 1 with Paisley University. I wondered who these tutors were who were called Learning Reps. Clearly teachers in the west paid more attention to the SEJ than in the east.

After doing the module 1, there was a feedback for the course session in Edinburgh at Moray Place and the need for more LRs was mentioned. Some of us asked what they were and registered an interest.

After I had finished the CT accreditation process and had a couple of months breather I enrolled to do the LR course.

I had been an EIS rep 3 times in the past. I am not a particularly "union" sort of person. I do not enjoy being involved in committees, etc but like to be involved in practical, direct work with other teachers.

It seemed like something I would enjoy doing, and something I know I am able to do reasonably well – i.e. giving help, information, advice, support to others.

My seconded role involves being out and about supporting pupils, teachers and schools in the area of using ICT for additional support needs, so I was used to being in this sort of "helpful/encouraging" role.

I'm also a Chartered teacher adviser and assessor and this is very useful for a learning rep, as a lot of queries concern this.

I've always engaged in a lot of CPD over the years as a matter of course, long before the "35 hours" so felt I could encourage people to see it as a natural thing to want to do as it can make the job much more interesting and satisfying – if you find the right sort of CPD opportunities to suit your situation.

I must also admit – having been out on secondment I feared being in one school again might feel claustrophobic. This was a chance to get out and about and engage with people out-with my own institution.

I was slightly surprised that I was accepted without any apparent checks being made on me or any selection process. I was welcomed, invited to a meeting of new reps even before I started on the course. But that was useful, though I still wasn't entirely sure exactly what I would be expected to do' (Personal Record 5).

A key point that comes out of the above explanations is that the remit for their day job means the respondents will come into contact with many colleagues and they have stated that this is an obvious advantage to them as a LR. It would seem sensible for the EIS and other stakeholders to use this evidence to encourage other EIS members to consider taking on the role of LR.

The following respondent who volunteered to write a personal record provides another reason as to why members of this cohort of LRs volunteered and again shows the draw of such a role to members who have never been active in the Institute:

'I saw the advert inviting applicants to become L Reps just after a colleague had asked for support in writing and presenting an award bearing module. I found the experience rewarding and responding to the advert seemed appropriate. I had never before been an active union member although I come from a background of active union membership.

Because my work in the Area Network Support Service involves visiting various primary schools in the authority, the idea of becoming a multi-establishment L Rep appealed to me' (Personal Record 6).

The final respondent (who wrote a personal record) volunteered to become a LR because firstly the Institute had stood by him and represented him when he had been in dispute with his local authority in relation to a campaign he was involved in to stop school closures. This led him to become active in his local association to give something back to the union and when a ME LR position was required to be filled he took up the challenge as further payback to the Institute. Secondly, because he was Chartered Teacher qualified and thirdly '...*to make the biggest difference*' (Personal Record 7).

Karen Gilmore pointed out that as part of her students' induction process she asks them why they want to be LRs and she highlighted the following answers as being the key reasons why they volunteer:

- There is no information out there on CPD;
- The prospective LRs have found difficulty in getting CPD information;
- Encountering problems as to interpretation at school and local authority level as to what CPD means;
- The prospective LRs have found that some schools have a broad definition of CPD in that it is continuing professional and personal development whilst others state that if CPD is not tied into the school plan then teachers will not be allowed to undertake CPD activities;
- Some of the prospective LRs feel threatened by CPD Co-ordinators
- Some of the prospective LRs have stated that the CPD they have received has been "rubbish" and that they have been sent on courses that are "death by powerpoint" with no relevance and little transferability in relation to their day-to-day work (Gilmore, 2007).

The final point could have the following implications. Firstly, if this situation is endemic within the Scottish education sector then it has as Wojecki (2007: 1-3) describes a significant number of "wounded learners" that have experienced "wounding learning practices". Wojecki (2007: 2) expands upon this as follows:

'Individuals wounded through learning are not lacking in their capacity for learning, but rather, through their experiences, it is one's relationships to learning which may be wounded. This is to say that the learner's relationship to learning has been injured, and through this injured relationship the learner's identities to learning and their vocational trajectories may be impacted...

...Irregardless of how this injurious story or experience has been sustained, whether by peers, educators, the institution, the workplace, or the curricula, it leaves an indelible mark on the psyche of the learner because they are inherently linked with and attached to the individual's experiences and concepts of learning. These negative and emotive experiences thus continue to shape how the individual "knows what learning is, therefore, framing how the individual engages with formal learning and training programs in the future. These injurious experiences shape the motivations and personal justifications for their avoidance, resistance, emotional responses, and non-engagement with formal learning activities'.

Secondly, this may be a reason why teachers do not seek advice and guidance from the LRs.

Karen pointed out when analysing why the students wish to become LRs, two types seem to emerge, the "cynical" and the "evangelists". The cynics argue that current CPD provision is irrelevant and something needs to be done about it, whilst the evangelists are very enthusiastic about CPD and its accrued benefits. She went on to state that there is a correlation between those students who have completed CT or are doing CT and those who are the evangelists. It is as if they are saying that CPD has changed my life and I can also bring it to you (Gilmore, 2007).

The next chapter will examine the level of support this cohort has received.

6

Supporting the Learning Representatives

Introduction

As indicated above this chapter will analyse how the LRs are being supported by the Institute and other stakeholders at local level. Support at this level is imperative if the LRs are to become accepted and embedded within local authority and school CPD structures.

The Integration of the Learning Representatives into Local Association Structures

The LRs were asked if they had been fully integrated into their local association structure and the answers are a cause for concern. In relation to the ME LRs, six (50%) stated they had been whilst the other 50% stated they had not. Of those who answered in the affirmative, the following indicative examples are:

'I am also LA Secretary…I was fairly well integrated before I became L Rep…Partly. We have use of the LA office during our 0.5fte LR time, and we sometimes have the opportunity to speak to our LA Secretary while there. Have been made to feel welcome. So far we've had one article in the EIS Newsletter…I report to the Local Association'.

A similar picture emerges from the responses of the School LRs. Nine (45%) stated that they had been fully integrated into their local association structure, whilst the slight majority, eleven (55%) stated they had not. Of those who answered in the affirmative, the following examples are indicative of their experiences:

'Ongoing regular meetings/input…Regular invitations to events. Plans afoot for all LRs to meet up'.

The personal records echo the explanations of both the ME and School LRs. Six of the personal records alluded to the LRs relationship with their respective local associations and in five cases the relationship is very positive although in one case it was noted that the Local Association Secretary has been a little slow in agreeing time-off with the local authority for the LR (Personal

Record 5). The following two explanations are examples of the positive relationship that the respective LRs have with their local association:

'I have had a very supportive experience from my LA Management committee who were fully aware of the potential impact of the role' (Personal Record 4).

'As I have had no previous involvement with my Local Association, I asked to meet them, was invited along, introduced to the committee and I feel I could turn to them if required' (Personal Record 6).

The following explanation from one of the personal records although positive still shows that there is work to be done:

'Accepted by Local Association...Yes – member of the executive – dealing with some queries – still lack of understanding to some extent of Learning Rep role and time off they need for casework compared to time off required by other reps' (Personal Record 7).

The responses from both the questionnaire and the personal records indicate that the LRs who have had previous or current experience of being an EIS representative are more likely to be embedded within their local association structures.

However, this raises the question as to how the new and inexperienced activists are accepted and ingratiated into the local structures. Donnelly and Kiely (2007; 5) have found that the ULRs involved in their evaluation:

'...recognise a continuum between learning activism at one extreme and branch activism at the other, nonetheless they differ as to where they choose to locate themselves on such a spectrum, when invited to do so...a polarisation emerges based on background such that those new to activism tend to define themselves more narrowly by reference to learning than other "mainstream" union issues compared to those taking on learning representation in addition to their other branch roles. Some new "learning activists" even report themselves as rarely attending formal branch forums or partaking in broader branch activities'.

The participants were then asked if they reported their activities at local association meetings and again the responses should give cause for concern. The evidence comes in the main from the questionnaires as only one respondent who completed a personal record commented on this issue. In relation to the ME

LRs eight (66.7%) stated that they reported their activities whilst four (33.3%) stated they did not. Three of the respondents added an additional explanation. The first participant, who answered in the affirmative stated that they did report most of their activities except '...confidential matters relating to individual members', which is reasonable whilst the second respondent who also answered in the affirmative stated that they reported their activities to the local association not as a LR but as a local delegate. This answer should be of concern to the EIS as all LRs should be able to report their activities to their local association as a matter of right as LRs and in no other capacity. The third respondent who answered in the negative stated 'Not yet. One of us went to a council meeting and explained what we do'.

The situation for the School LRs is less positive as only three (15%) stated that they reported their activities whilst the overwhelming majority, seventeen (85%) did not. Significantly, not one of the respondents who answered in the negative expanded on their answers.

The one respondent who dealt with this issue in their personal record stated that:

'There are 2 of us so far in Edinburgh. My colleague has addressed the local executive meeting to explain what we do.

We've been a bit slow in getting organised but will soon take turns at going to Rep meetings to share what we've been doing and get up to date with their issues.

We have been recommended by other LRs to join the executive but neither feels we have the time to take on any more commitments at present' (Personal Record 5).

An interesting development in the support of LRs was highlighted by Karen Gilmore who pointed out changes to the LRs training courses now meant that student LRs were being paired up with accredited and experienced LRs (Gilmore, 2007). This coaching/mentoring approach can do only good and ensures that new LRs are assimilated into the structures of the Institute at a much earlier stage. It can be regarded as a significant step forward and will hopefully allow LRs to become embedded within the union, particularly at local association level.

Learning Representatives Experiences of Being Accepted by their Headteacher/s

The first study found that very few headteachers understood the role and responsibilities of LRs and those that did were not particularly accepting or supportive of them. This sub-section will examine how the LRs' relationship with headteachers has developed to date.

In respect of being accepted by their headteacher(s) overall the situation looks positive for both sets of LRs, more so for the ME LRs. In relation to the ME LRs nine (75%) stated that they had been accepted; two (16.7%) stated they had not and one participant (8.3%) did not answer the question. Of those that answered in the affirmative, the following examples are an indication of the relationship they have with their headteacher:

'My headteacher understands the position however formal time-off has not been reached with the region...Good supportive working relationship though not sure he understands my role...HT very keen on post of LR... My headteacher supports my role as EIS L.R. She is prepared to allow flexible timetable on my part to attend EIS LR business'.

Of the participants who answered in the negative they explained why this was the case as following indicative answers illustrate:

'My role is rarely acknowledged by my line manager other than to query expenses that may be related. I have to request slots to disseminate CPD information...Not accepted by Local Authority, so headteacher not interested'.

As for the participant who did not answer the question they gave the following explanation:

'I don't really have a headteacher, as I'm on secondment. The people I work with have little interest in what I do'.

This is an interesting answer in that this may well indicate apathy or even hostility towards the role of LRs and was examined further in the primary research phase.

In relation to the School LRs the situation is positive but there are concerns. Twelve (60%) stated they had been accepted by their headteacher; seven (35%) indicated they had not and one participant (5%) indicated the question was not applicable to them. Of the LRs that answered in the affirmative, the following examples are indicative of their relationship with their headteacher:

'Fully supportive – values collegiality and leadership development... Current HT accepts my role, but sometimes expects me to over contribute to her role as CPD Coordinator which I am not! Does accept my position however...Feel valued for advice. Supportive of LR role – though no extra time allowed for duties...Small School – Daily conversation/ inclusion in decisions...Very positive'

The LRs that indicated they did not have a relationship with their headteacher gave the following explanations:

'Since I moved to my new post/school I have not been recognised as the "official school LR by EIS group or therefore by HT...Since I became an LR, there have been many upheavals – The school had a change of HT and my timetable has been altered, allowing very little time for LR duties in the school...Still not given any time or recognition by head teacher...Not interested in my "role" doesn't see it as a "role". If I'm honest I'm not sure what my role is either...Headteacher saw no need for L Rep as he felt committed to promote the CPD Co-ordinator'

Two respondents took the opportunity to expand on issues highlighted in the questionnaire and both wrote about their experiences within their own establishments focussing on the problems of dealing with senior management as the following comments show:

'I am very disappointed that the powers that be in the schools are not willing to involve anyone else in the matter of teachers' personal and professional development. I have failed utterly to change anything as they seem to guard jealously their control, asking only for vague ideas from staff as to what they want for the coming year. Despite union recognition, few staff are aware of my training.

As I am on secondment in this school, I am in an outsider's position anyway. But my base school was very unwelcoming of the idea that non-management should have any meaningful input; I moved soon after I qualified as LR.

We have a multi-establishment LR in the region, I am the only establishment-based LR and I feel I am superfluous'

'I must say that it would be much easier for LRs to do their duties if an agreement was set out and given to Headteacher.

This would clarify and make the LR more comfortable as a working partnership between LRs and school would already be established.

I am currently negotiating for some time out of class to undertake my LR duties. I can understand how difficult it is to provide cover.

I have already discussed the matter with [a local association officer] *— I said I would let him know.*

My HT has spoken to [a local association officer] *and told me… that LR may obtain 0.1 but this has not been confirmed yet'*

As these comments indicate, while progress has been made with some headteachers there are a number who have yet to realise the benefits and potential of LRs in relation to their schools' CPD strategies and are not cognisant of their legal obligations in relation to time-off and facilities. This situation was highlighted by the respondents who completed personal records. Five of the respondents wrote about the issue and three of the comments were negative and two were positive. The comments indicate more effort has to be put in by both headteachers and LRs to ensure that the former understand the latter's role and responsibilities and personal relationships do play a significant factor as the following examples indicate:

'My own management team do very little to support the [LR] *role. If I ask for slots at meetings to take the opportunity to promote a forthcoming event, the request is either denied or forgotten. I used to persist in attempting to promote my role with my managers but am aware I only do so occasionally now'* (Personal Record 6).

'…My headteacher was very supportive as he saw the role of LR complementing PRD by encouraging staff to plan and focus on Professional Development' (Personal Record 3).

The final comment shows how relationships with headteachers can be positive and the final part of this section will be a case study of a head teacher who values the role of LRs. Alasdair Macdonald is the headteacher of Johnstone High School, Renfrewshire, and has known about LRs from virtually the start. He understands their role to be about essentially encouraging EIS members to participate in CPD and to offer advice and ways forward on CPD. Alasdair believes that the LRs operate within the context of the school's and local authority's CPD policies and emphasised that they are not an alternative to these policies (Macdonald, 2007).

Alasdair's initial contact with LRs was through the authority's ME LR who happened to teach at his school and when asked how the LRs fit into the current school and local authority CPD structures and that there was no conflict. He stated that he interprets the role of the LR is to encourage teachers to avail themselves of CPD opportunities and to give advice on CPD be it either on a one-day course or Masters in Education. The LR is not seen as part of the management structure so there is not the managerialist element to the role (Macdonald, 2007).

When asked about how the LRs "fit" within the system and the school, Alasdair stated that in theory it is about right and overall the LR role is in keeping with the *McCrone Agreement*. He stated the LR he has most contact with is enthusiastic but this enthusiasm is not always taken on-board by teachers to get out of school and into CPD. Alasdair argued there is still an anti-academic attitude that prevails amongst teachers and pointed out if this mindset is not overcome then both CPD and Professional Review and Development (PRD) initiatives will not take off as anticipated and expected by the strategic stakeholders. He argued:

'I see that PRD is about a discourse between professionals that leads to CPD and the LR is important in helping to overcome this cynicism and apprehension in terms of the anti-academic attitude. There is a fear of the unknown in terms of taking on CPD and possibly being found out. The teachers should be reflective intelligent enquirers into their own practice' (Macdonald, 2007).

Based on his own experience Alasdair was asked to differentiate between the roles of school and authority based CPD QIOs and Co-ordinators and LRs. He began by arguing that if a head teacher has the courage of devolving responsibility to CPD Co-ordinators within schools this is a positive move as they have greater autonomy post-*McCrone*. Alasdair went on to point out that to some extent there is an issue between local authorities and schools as the ideas authorities are putting forward pertaining to CPD, are not addressing what schools and headteachers see as meeting their own needs. The authorities do not have the level of exposure or numbers to advise teachers on CPD, post-disaggregation of the Scottish regional authorities. Thus it is now for School CPD Co-ordinators to look at *'… what does our school require'* and to provide opportunities for staff to be able to fulfil the needs of the school (Macdonald, 2007).

Alasdair pointed out that the School CPD Co-ordinator is not acting autonomously as they are part of the strategy and dialogue of the different parties within a school. He added that due to the industrial disputes of the 1970s and 1980s and the '...*Michael Forsyth mindset*' this has produced a very defensive mindset amongst secondary school teachers and it manifests itself in an '...*oppositionist attitude*' in that '...*we are not doing it*', particularly in relation to CPD. Alasdair continued by highlighting a paradox, in that a number of teachers in the past three decades have been innovative in helping to bring in initiatives, for example the introduction of standard grades and *Higher Still* (Macdonald, 2007).

He argued what *McCrone* tried to do (and schools and headteachers have) was to liberate the creativeness of teachers but within a framework. Alasdair stated this is the position that schools and head teachers are in and they are trying to motivate teachers to become creative. He pointed out it is also about senior managers needing to be more creative about managing their professionals, particularly Deputes and Principal Teachers by allowing them to bring in initiatives and be creative and this is where LRs can play a key role. Alasdair believes that LRs are there to break down barriers and the opposition that he previously mentioned. He readily admits that there is pressure on LRs as they are seen somewhere between the union and management (Macdonald, 2007).

Alasdair pointed out that, in its history, the EIS at national level has been very innovative. It has always had a strong professional role but it is also a trade union that has to defend its members. It has to deal with this paradox and tension which in turns transfers down to the LRs who have to deal with the arguments that teachers cannot undertake professional development due to it being a workload issue, when in fact it is not and they do have the capacity to do it (Macdonald, 2007).

He stated that he has a sound working relationship with the LR who is based at his school. The way in which he sees working together with the LR is for the LR to allay the fears and win the hearts and minds of teachers in relation to professional development. In turn, it is for Alasdair and his team to work in tandem with the LR by not being too heavy handed in relation to professional development and working in partnership with the LR to promote professional development (Macdonald, 2007).

Alasdair feels his school has benefited in terms of working with the LR as the LR has helped to start changing the mindset of teachers; build trust; promote professional values and the courage to express these values in public (Macdonald, 2007). He stated that he will continue to work with the LR in the same vein as it is about changing attitudes and this takes time. Alasdair explained that many of the "veterans" of the industrial disputes he alluded to earlier were coming up for retirement and moving out of the profession having done a good educational job but helping to create the oppositionist mindset within the staffroom. He believes that this mindset will die away as new people come in with whom he is impressed, and that Initial Teacher Education is one of the success stories of *McCrone*. Alasdair feels that this change will make the LR's job easier in terms of pushing the professional development agenda forward (Macdonald, 2007). This view runs in parallel with the findings of Audit Scotland and HMIE in terms of the younger generation of teachers being more inclined to take up CPD and CT opportunities.

Alasdair felt that the LR has had a positive impact and states that:

'...the impact has been on individuals who have been willing to approach the LR and then embarked on, for example, Chartered Teacher modules/programme. The hope is that a significant number of individuals adopt this approach and hopefully in the future the ethos of teachers will become more professional due in part to the advice and guidance they have received from the LR' (Macdonald, 2007).

In terms of raising the profile of the LR, Alasdair was of the opinion that it was a matter for the EIS locally. He stated that, at local level, the EIS must strike a balance between promoting professional development and defending the rights of teachers. It has got to promote CPD not solely as *'something done to teachers'* but as an area where teachers can be creative, innovative and self-generating. He concluded by stating that he believed it is *'...about telling teachers to be intelligent self-enquirers into their own pedagogic practice'* (Macdonald, 2007).

The chapter will continue by addressing time-off and funded cover arrangements for this cohort of LRs. These are key elements to consider as, in the first study, time-off was highlighted as a problem. If this cohort of LRs is to be effective then it is imperative that appropriate time-off and funded cover facilities have been afforded them and agreed and signed up to between the local authority and local association.

Time-Off Arrangements for the Learning Representatives

The LRs were asked if their local authority had agreed time-off arrangements for them and the results highlight a great disparity between ME and School LRs which should cause significant concern amongst the key stakeholders. Eight (66.7%) of the ME LRs had a formal time-off agreement in place, whilst four (33.3%) indicated they did not. Of the LRs that did not have arrangements, the following examples are indicative as to why this was the case:

'It has been agreed but the director has not sent a letter to my headteacher confirming this. Until this happens time-off is not a formal arrangement...Authority obfuscating instead of negotiating by asking for more details. I have provided Secretary with heaps of documents to bombard them with and await developments...They generally arrange meetings to discuss this and then cancel at the last minute (Head of Schools). EIS not proactive enough either...The LA Secretary has not asked for time off'.

The participants were given the opportunity to make additional comments and the following comment should cause further concern for the stakeholders:

'At present I feel in limbo. Until I get a letter from the director formally acknowledging my position my hands are tied. (I was told a number of months ago he was going to write it!)...Despite all of this I'm still very positive about the future of the EIS LR prog.'

As indicated above the situation in relation to the School LRs is far more negative as only four (20%) have arrangements in place whilst sixteen (80%) do not. Of the overwhelming majority of School LRs that do not have any type of agreement in place the following explanations are indicative of why this is the case:

'As I have no reason to need time-off, I have asked for none...I haven't requested time-off, due to above! [due to the participant's negative relationship with their head teacher]*...Still formulating a policy... Supply cover costs...Haven't heard from LA...No formal agreement yet with EIS. HT not willing to give time off without agreement from EIS. Although recently I approached my HT about being a multi-rep, she had not heard about time for this also and did say 30 mins per week would be better but as yet have not had any time to develop my LR duties.I felt this would cause internal problems in my school as L Reps are not seen as a priority.'*

Two key factors emerge from the above negative responses. Firstly, it shows the inexperience of the School LRs as nine out of the thirteen who expanded on their negative answers have never held a union post before. Thus the EIS at both national and local level has work to do in terms of educating and supporting these representatives so they are able to carry out their role actively. Secondly, these answers should be a cause for concern as the LRs have a legal entitlement to time-off and facilities. The fact that a number of them do not think they need it seems surprising at the very least and added to local associations not helping or recognising LRs should be a cause for concern. Wallis et al. (2005: 296) may have part of the answer for this in their study of ULRs as they found that:

'...some ULRs have not sought to negotiate with their employers because they lacked the necessary skills and experience, whilst others who are already bargaining with employers, even on an informal basis, may need to develop additional skills in order to maximise their effectiveness'.

Overall, five of the respondents who completed personal records dealt with this issue and four of them were positive on this issue. Their following comments can act as examples of best practice when dealing with this issue at both national and local level:

'To date, time-off for LR work has been arranged within non-contact hours or outwith school day...Negotiation will be required if extending the role next year' (Personal Record 2).

'The Local Authority and my direct line-manager were enlightened enough to see the benefits of allocating me dedicated facility time because of what they were getting in return from me... [as a]..."value-added" resource. This is in addition to all the other EIS work I need time for. It actually worked out cheaper to pay a teacher for three days than to pay for ad hoc days, afternoons and mornings!' (Personal Record 4).

'I am allocated half a day per week for L Rep duties and find this can be used quite flexibly for visits, research, meetings etc. I often visit teachers after the school day' (Personal Record 6).

'25 days off seemingly funded from general supply budget...Authority were slow to agree the time but will be prepared to review it in the coming spring. I suspect I will settle for the same again for next year as I continue to find my feet and consider whether I am up to the task' (Personal Record 7).

Whilst there are examples of good practice as highlighted by the above examples there is a problem with time-off in relation to a number of this second cohort of EIS LRs. However, at national level, the Institute's view is that in the overwhelming majority of cases time-off has been satisfactorily negotiated. The following explanation by Lyn McClintock, seems to be at odds with the day-to-day experiences of certain members of this second cohort:

'One of the major issues which has occupied me has been the issue of time off for LRs. In the main the issues over time off for multi-establishment LRs have been resolved and it is now easier to get time off arrangements in place for new LRs' (McClintock, 2007:1).

Lyn along with one of the respondents (Personal Record 1) does point out that there are outstanding time-off cases based on a lack of support from local associations. However, as she states this situation will not arise in the future as:

'...the LR Protocol is now being strictly adhered to and a Confirmation of Approval Form must be received together with the LR course application form signed and dated by the relevant person. I have to say that if this practice had been in place right at the start we would not have as many new activists within the EIS as I suspect that local associations would only support people they knew and new people would have found it almost impossible to receive approval. Given the fact that a lot of LRs are now active within their local association executive and attending AGMs etc the EIS could have been deprived of "new blood" which every union requires along with the continuity of experienced union members' (McClintock, 2007:1).

The next observation will show the EIS is not totally convinced that time-off agreements are working in practice, particularly with School LRs:

'Once the first cohort of school LRs were accredited discussions began both at authority level and school level to obtain time off for them to undertake the LR role. To date the average time off negotiated for school LRs is one period per week. Time off in general has been agreed quite readily for school LRs and may be a sign that there is more awareness of the role. However a survey is currently being carried out of all school LRs to establish whether or not the time off agreement is only on paper or whether they are actually receiving the time off allocated. One of the school LRs devised an Action Plan which had assisted in

her being granted time off and this was included in the LR Handbook'
(McClintock, 2007: 2).

The evidence presented above indicates that the formal time-off agreements in place for School LRs are not working in practice. The EIS at national level is right to be concerned as the majority of School LRs are: not being allowed to carry out their role and responsibilities; being discouraged at local level from being active; do not have enough time to discharge their duties and having to carry out their role in their own time.

The key stakeholders at local authority and school level should also be concerned as the law is clearly being broken in many instances. Additionally, a public consultation on workplace representatives (which included LRs) and a review of their facilities and facility time initiated by the then (UK) Department for Trade and Industry (DTI) (2007) took place last year and the results of UK Government's response to it were published in November 2007 by the Department for Business Enterprise & Regulatory Reform (BERR and formerly the DTI) (2007). It will not make happy reading for local authorities and school management in Scotland. Whilst the UK Government stopped short of strengthening the *Employment Act* 2002 (Parliament, 2002), (which is the primary legislation pertaining to LRs) it did make the following recommendations:

'The ACAS [Advisory, Conciliation and Arbitration Service] Code of Practice on Time Off for Trade Union Activities should be revised and updated. The Government will ask Acas to consider how the issues of cover, workloads, the position of managers, access to ICT facilities and confidentiality should be treated in its Code...

...A new training tool should be devised to assist and encourage employers to help line managers to work constructively with those workplace representatives in their teams...

...The Government intends to issue a joint declaration with trade unions and employer organisations describing the role of modern representatives and the positive contribution they make to the workplace.

The Government would encourage other organisations to draft similar statements of their own geared to their own circumstances. For example, the Government will ask the Public Services Forum to consider drafting a statement expressing support for the activities of modern representatives working in public services and the contribution they are making for their customers. This might include examples of good practice...

...The Government notes that many facilities agreements between employers and trade unions are out of date. The Government recommends that employers and trade unions re-examine their existing agreements once the Acas Code of Practice has been revised...

The Government has decided to retain the existing legal status of the Acas Code of Practice...

...The Government considers it important that representatives should be able to harness the power of ICT equipment to communicate effectively with the people they represent and to make best use of their scarce time off...the Government considers that Acas should consider revising the Code of Practice by providing greater guidance on facilities, especially the use of ICT equipment and the security of communications by representatives. The revision of the Code should act as a spur for individual organisations to review existing facilities agreements, and the Government contends that old agreements should be brought up to date by employers and their recognised unions' (BERR, 2007: 2-4).

These recommendations are not only self-explanatory but will impact on the Scottish education system when they are incorporated and introduced. It would be wise of local authorities and school management to ensure that they abide by these recommendations by acting upon them before they come into operation.

Funded Cover for the Learning Representatives

The participants were asked if funded cover was being provided by their local authority for their activities as LRs and again the answers make for disturbing reading. Five (41.7%) ME LRs stated that their local authority provided funded cover for their activities; five (41.7%) stated their local authority did not; one participant stated that they did not know and another indicated that they were in a strange position due to their secondment. In relation to the LRs that have no funded cover, the following explanations are indicative as to why this is the case:

'Don't have a job that usually gets cover as not class committed...My secondment is funded by the support for learning central budget. They are happy to save 0.1 of my salary as they would have preferred only to fund me part time in any case...I carry out duties in my "free" time'

As for the School LRs the situation is less positive. Only two (10%) stated they had funded cover, whilst one (5%) was unsure and seventeen (85%) indicated they had no funded cover. Of the LRs that had no funded cover, the following explanations are indicative as to why this was the case as follows:

'Can only be released when staffing in school permits...I have time out of class anyway – I use this time for LR duties/meetings...I do this as part of CPD in own time – with co-operation of staff too...I have chosen to use one of my own preparation/non-contact periods as my time-off. This is in order that my colleagues do not receive "please takes" for one of my classes...I do this sort of thing in my own time – lack of suitable supply staff. I only leave my class if what I do will directly benefit them because my absence can be a disaster!'

The final comment was made by a Special Needs teacher and indicates the particular issues specialist teachers face in the role of LR. The above negative explanations also re-emphasise the point made in relation to inexperience, as nine out of the thirteen comments came from LRs who had never held a union position before.

Only two of the respondents who completed personal records dealt with this issue. One had no problem but another highlighted a practical factor that some specialist teachers may find in a number of authorities as the following explanation will highlight:

'Finding science teachers locally is a problem. I had one lined-up but she got a full time job on the neighbouring island. Someone else has agreed in principle for the days from October to Christmas' (Personal Record 7).

Local authorities and school management should be concerned about this issue as, in the previous section, it was highlighted that the current Acas Code of Practice (2003) will be revised and deal with funded cover for LRs. It would be advisable that employers in the Scottish education system tackle the problems in relation to funded cover for LRs before they are forced to under the revised code. Failure to do so may result in legal action being taken against them. This may well prove to be embarrassing as both the Scottish and UK Governments have publicly praised the work of LRs and have encouraged employers and unions to work closer together to promote the lifelong learning agenda through the use of LRs.

The next chapter will examine the developing working relationship and partnership between the LRs and their local authority and school CPD counterparts.

7

Developing Partnership Working

Introduction

This chapter will examine the working relationship and growing partnership between Local Authority CPD QIOs and School CPD Co-ordinators, with particular emphasis on the former. It will highlight how through one activity this relationship has begun to blossom and drawn teachers into taking up professional development activities.

Developing Partnership Working with LA CPD QIOs

The participants were asked if they were working in partnership with their LA CPD QIOs (sometimes referred to as CPD Co-ordinators) and the ME LRs. Eight (66.7%) stated that they were and four (33.3%) stated they were not. The following examples are illustrative of some of the partnership working that is taking place:

'Share platforms, planning, joint working, regular meetings... We received a lot of info on how to operate. They have been very cooperative. We meet about twice a term. It was with head of CPD but now with the new "Teachers' CPD" person. We're invited to events and contribute to CPD Bulletins – and have so far put in 3 articles. We have jointly set up a CT network and are planning a CT "Fair" for prospective CTs and providers in May.'

These are positive responses which show the barriers that were in place in relation to the first cohort of ME LRs are beginning to be removed and there is a far more positive relationship based on joint working, mutual understanding and partnership. The initial findings merited further investigation and these positive developments will be analysed below in greater depth.

Improving the Working Relationship with LA CPD QIOs

To examine further why there has been such a positive shift in the relationship between the ME LRs and the LA CPD QIOs, a number of these officers were interviewed. In total six QIOs were interviewed who worked for five local education authorities geographically spread throughout Scotland. In one case, two officers were interviewed from the same authority due to the different and interesting nature of their interaction with their LR counterparts.

All the officers were asked to explain what they understood to be the role of the EIS LRs and the following selection of explanations are indicative of their understanding:

'I understand that they are staff side advice and guidance for all teachers (not just EIS members) in relation to professional development, particularly Chartered Teacher' (LA CPD QIO 2 Interview).

'The role of the EIS LR is as a point of contact within the authority and with teachers at all levels who will get advice and guidance on the CPD opportunities available to them and that will meet their needs' (LA CPD QIO 5 Interview).

'To promote learning amongst all fellow teachers, not just EIS members and also to facilitate access to CPD in its widest context and the promotion of Chartered Teacher' (LA CPD QIO 6 Interview).

One officer discussed the ME LRs in greater detail and observed how effective these individuals were depended on the quality of the individual. She stated that in her authority the ME LRs are *'...very committed and very supportive of her and her team'*. The QIO felt this close working relationship benefited teachers in schools. However, the positive aspects of the relationship were tempered somewhat by other observations as the officer felt that one of the ME LRs she dealt with was not as efficient as the others and had on occasion given wrong information which worried her (LA CPD QIO 1 Interview).

The QIO felt that more could probably be done with the ME LRs if they had satisfactory communication skills and relevant teaching experience (both in terms of length of service and subject areas). She also stated that if there were more ME LRs within the authority it would be of benefit as they could further support her and her team as they are short-staffed. The officer pointed out it is only recently (after what can be termed the "bedding-in" period) that she and her team have seen the ME LRs do something positive with their half-day for LR duties. She has asked the LRs to talk to teachers on the General Teaching Council of Scotland's (GTCS)

Framework for Professional Development. She went on to state that they '…*are doing more of this now and what a difference it makes as they have a role now*' as the officer sees it (LA CPD QIO 1 Interview).

The above answers indicate that the officers have a clear understanding of the role of the LRs and that partnership working is in place. It is also significant that overall this working relationship is positive, the QIOs are welcoming of the support of the LRs and see scope for the role of the LR to grow. Alexandrou (2006; 2007) has outlined how the EIS LRs are selected and the standards and protocols they must observe. However, the EIS at national level must ensure its quality assurance procedures in relation to the selection, training and accreditation of LRs are such that the LRs maintain a quality of service that does not undermine the whole initiative. Thus, ongoing training is essential as more is demanded of the ME LRs and the stronger their working relationship becomes with their local authority counterparts.

Based on their experiences and observations the officers were asked how the LRs "fitted" into their respective authority's CPD structures. One of the QIOs stated a ME LRs attends the authority's CPD Extended Team meeting and she and the LRs had recently been involved in planning and delivering a CPD event. The officer pointed out that this group has had five planning meetings to date for the event and not only was she advising the LRs, she would also have a part to play on the day of the event (LA CPD QIO 1 Interview).

The officer stated this event was more about the ME LRs as they needed a higher profile within the authority as she was of the opinion that they do not have a high profile within schools. The QIO pointed out that it has been difficult for the ME LRs to get into schools unless it has been for a specific reason. She also stated that the LRs '…*have not been involved* [at school level]…*or welcomed partly because school managers are so busy*' (LA CPD QIO 1 Interview).

Other officers stated:

'*They fit in well, there are only three LRs who have spread themselves about. I meet with the LRs once or twice a term to share current practice about what I do and in turn the LRs share their experiences and they highlight issues which they have identified in schools which is extremely useful*' (LA CPD QIO 3 Interview).

This officer stated the LRs can be honest with her, for example, if she has rolled out an initiative they will give her their honest opinion on an initiative with comments on how well it is working or not. The QIO added the LRs are not breaking any confidences when they are sharing their views and highlighting issues with her (LA CPD QIO 3 Interview).

Whilst another explained:

'I meet monthly with [the LR]. *We both worked together to set up a Chartered Teacher Network that is for the promotion of Chartered Teacher and to encourage others* [to take up CT]. *This is working because teachers have come on board and she* [the LR] *liaises with the universities. She invites them to come to the authority and gives presentations to the teachers on their Chartered Teacher programmes.*

We have organised annually a CPD event and it was her idea. We ran it for a third time in May of this year and the event has got bigger. More teachers attend each year and [the LR] *helps me organise this event. This event was over-subscribed – standing room only…* [the LR] *is totally committed to this event, CPD and working in partnership with me and the authority. As the lead officer for CPD it is good for me to have such a dedicated and enthusiastic individual. It is like working with a peer and her commitment is unparalled.* [The LR] *has a different perspective that complements my work'* (LA CPD QIO 6 Interview).

This officer went on to state that the LR he works with helps him in relation to the teacher networks and other initiatives he has set up and instigated including the Cooperative Learning Academies training sessions run by the authority. He pointed out that the:

'EIS has helped me by getting attendance at these academies and raising teachers' awareness about their obligations under the 21ˢᵗ Century Agreement. This has been due to the activities of both the EIS LR and the EIS Local Association. I truly believe that this is a strong partnership between myself and the EIS and is a relationship of trust' (LA CPD QIO 6 Interview).

The above comments show how the ME LRs are becoming embedded within the CPD structures of local authorities. They are building up strong meaningful partnerships and working relationships with their CPD QIO counterparts that are bearing fruit not only in terms of organising and delivering CPD events but also by engaging and encouraging more teachers to take up CPD activities.

Further evidence of this embedding comes in the form of the two stakeholders working together on CPD related working groups and committees. This will be dealt with in greater detail in one of the following sub-sections.

The officers were asked whether the EIS LRs' "fit" is right or if improvements can be made and their answers make for interesting reading as the following comments indicate:

'Improvements can be made. I think it would be useful to have examples of best practice as to how local authorities and learning representatives are working together' (LA CPD QIO 2 Interview).

'I think the current practice is working well and we have to allow it to develop. What we have done is not run before we could walk and we have gradually talked about areas where we could work together' (LA CPD QIO 3 Interview).

'Improvements can always be made. The role is developing further and because of [the LR's] *work and commitment she has been promoted to a...post within the authority with a specific CPD remit'* (LA CPD QIO 6 Interview).

This officer went on to state that he wanted the LR out of the classroom for most of the week to carry out the duties of this post. However, the LR is a specialist subject teacher and teachers in her specialism are thin on the ground thus she cannot be replaced at the present time so is only able to have two days out of the classroom (LA CPD QIO 6 Interview). This raises the interesting issue of considering the opportunity costs for scarce skilled staff who happen to be LRs. This issue was not considered as part of this study but will be addressed in future evaluations. The QIO added that the LR is a good listener and:

'...LRs are part of the partnership approach to CPD and the LRs need to be given time to talk to teachers and build up the partnership approach. Trust is very important and this should be an element in the LRs "fit". [The LR] *has modelled CPD through being a LR. She is quick to take part in council initiatives and has also become a CT'* (LA CPD QIO 6 Interview).

Significantly, one of the officers argued that she did not believe the EIS LRs would have a long-term future unless they have a niche and the niche should be developing and supporting CPD. She felt for this to succeed the EIS needed to ensure it had capable representatives in place and much depends on the individual LR and the quality of this individual. Additionally, the QIO argued there should be a LRs selection policy to ensure good quality LRs and this would make a positive difference (LA CPD QIO 1 Interview). This might suggest this particular officer seems to have come across one or more ME LRs that may be less capable. This is a situation that the EIS at national level must monitor as any decline in the quality of the LRs and the advice, guidance and support they give to colleagues may well undermine the LRs initiative.

The officers were asked how and when they communicated with the LRs and if this was on a regular basis. The answers were extremely positive and showed there were several lines of communication open between the officers and the LRs; they met on a regular basis and the LRs have become embedded within the CPD structures of their respective authorities. Examples of how the QIOs and LRs meet include regular Extended Team Meetings; CPD Steering Group meetings; GLOW (the Scottish schools intranet, formerly known as the Scottish Schools Digital Network (SSDN)) Project Group meetings; termly and monthly meetings and planning meetings for CPD events.

One of the officers stated she and the LRs in her authority try and meet once or twice a term and often meet more as they jointly chair the local Chartered Teacher Network Groups. The QIO stated that in her authority 100 plus teachers were on the CT route and this is an area she foresaw the LRs helping her more with, particularly as they were understanding of her own heavy workload. Thus, together they have set up these networks and the LRs have divided up the authority area between them. They try and hold these network meetings once a term and the officer pointed out she and the LRs would be holding a series of meetings to decide on the future direction of these networks. Additionally, the QIO and the LRs will be working together to organise an event with other authorities to celebrate the success of teachers achieving CT accreditation, as well as those teachers going through CT and teachers sharing best practice The officer highlighted one more example of how often she is contact with the LRs by pointing out that they sit on a new CPD committee set up and run by the local university (LA CPD QIO 3 Interview).

The officers were asked how they currently work together with LRs to promote CPD. They reiterated that this was through the various CPD steering and other related working groups; organising CPD events and CT network groups. However, a number of the QIOs highlighted other activities. In one instance this has involved producing regular CPD newsletters and asking the LRs to organise and run a CT Providers Exhibition. One officer stated that the LRs were more than capable of being involved in this type of activity. She then went on to add that she could ask the LRs to do much more if they could prove they had the quality to undertake certain activities and felt that the upcoming CPD event she and the LRs had organised would be a springboard for future collaboration (CPD QIO 1 Interview).

The QIOs were asked if their relationship with the LRs could be improved upon and a number of them stated they felt they already had in place a positive working relationship while others felt more could be achieved as the following response indicates:

'Yes, I think it is being improved upon all the time as we get to know each other better and because [the LR] has become more confident, she is enthusiastic and has access to CPD courses and programmes relevant to teacher professional development.

[The LR] has brought to my attention the issue of well-being and professional development and she has something to offer here that is relevant. [The LR] is a classroom teacher herself and talks to the teachers. She knows the situation and may well be able to convince other teachers to take up CPD if it is linked to their well-being. Because [the LR] has gone through Chartered Teacher she has knowledge of the standards in Scottish education and understands the relevance of these standards to professional development. In turn she pushes colleagues to attain these standards' (LA CPD QIO 6 Interview).

The officers were then asked about their plans for working with the LRs in the future. Most reiterated that they would be working with the LRs much as they had been doing up to this juncture but others saw further opportunities for partnership working as follows:

'...in all areas of CPD there is potentially opportunities to work with the LRs. For example, I am currently working on a new leadership development initiative with the university and I see a possible role for the

LRs in this and other new initiatives' (LA CPD QIO 3 Interview).

'…anytime I am undertaking a new initiative that will impact on teachers' activities I will immediately seek out [the LR] *for her views'* (LA CPD QIO 4 Interview).

Based on their knowledge, the officers were asked what impact (if any) the LRs had made at authority level. In the majority of cases the QIOs stated it was too early and hard to measure the LRs' impact although there were no significant negative comments. Interestingly, there were positive comments in terms of a number of LRs having an impact on the QIO themselves as the following example shows:

'…at authority level [the LR] *is providing me with confidence to go forward with initiatives because* [the LR] *helps me ensure that there are no issues that will cause concern to the Authority, particularly in terms of setting out strategy and strategic documents that when they are disseminated to schools, the schools will not take exception to them. I have been impressed with the way* [the LR] *conducts herself, represents the membership and is very pragmatic'* (LA CPD QIO 4 Interview).

The QIOs were asked how they thought LRs could improve teachers' understanding of CPD and the benefits of CPD and the following answers are indicative of what they thought:

'I think learning representatives have to model excellence. If they are advocates of professional development within schools they have to be involved at a high level. They should be involved in: classroom-based research; professional reading and debate; leading collaborative enquiry; should be keeping websites up-to-date with relevant journal abstracts or CPD impact findings and generally they need to raise their game' (LA CPD QIO 2 Interview).

'…the LRs are working with teachers who want to do CPD and are in contact with the cynical teachers as well and the feedback I am receiving is that the LRs are sending out a clear message that CPD is an entitlement and that all teachers should participate' (LA CPD QIO 3 Interview).

The obvious inferences from such answers are that the LRs can increase their colleagues' understanding of CPD by being role models, achieving CT status and pushing the benefits of CPD in all its forms to teachers. If this is to be achieved it is obvious the QIOs would have even greater respect for them and would help to further cement the working relationship they have with the LRs.

Based on their observations the officers were asked how the profile of the LRs could be raised within their authority areas. A recurring answer was that the LRs should be involved in the local CT networks and continue with organising and delivering CPD events. It was also noted that their contact details should be placed on the authority websites and the EIS at national level should do more to promote and clarify the role of the LRs. Another suggestion was that:

'Learning representatives could be involved in mentoring younger or less experienced teachers and they should be visible at major CPD events. I would like to see regular contributions to our CPD course prospectus, website and discussion forum' (LA CPD QIO 2 Interview).

One of the officers encapsulated what it meant to be working with a LR as follows:

'The fact that she is very close to teachers and if issues arise I feel comfortable in discussing them with [the LR] and she is pro-active in sorting out problems before they become too difficult. The fact that the EIS has created LRs is great and they are helping teachers with their CPD and lifelong learning. [The LR] has her ear to the ground and is close to teachers and gets back to me with issues which we both work together to resolve.

You want to provide what is best and most relevant in relation to CPD and you can do it with LRs better than with the previous structures and this is hugely important. This is a good argument for keeping and developing them' (LA CPD QIO 6 Interview).

To highlight how positive the working relationship between the LRs and the officers has become at authority level, a recent initiative that has cemented the relationship between the two and managed to engage teachers with the professional development agenda will be examined.

The Organisation and Delivery of Joint CPD Events

In 2007, the EIS received funding from the Scottish Government to undertake further capacity building of its LRs initiative. The Institute has used this funding to promote the role of LRs as well as CPD and CT through the organisation and delivery of joint CPD events with local authorities. I have attended such events and observed first hand the positive impact they have had on the teachers who have attended them.

Although a relatively recent concept it was essential to understand the impact that these events were having in relation to the LRs; their relationship with LA CPD QIOs; members; outcomes and what the future strategy would be in relation to such events. Six of the LRs who were involved in organising these CPD events agreed to answer a questionnaire in relation to such events.

The participants were asked how the idea of a joint CPD event in their area came about. In four cases, such an event came about through the intervention of the EIS LR Administrator either in one-to one discussions with the relevant LRs or in meetings that included both the LRs and LA CPD QIOs. In the two other cases the LRs explained how the events came about as follows:

'Multi-Establishment LRs discussing ideas of improving our profile + meeting teachers as getting permission to get into schools was slow'.

'In discussion with the CPD coordinator when looking into ways which the LA and EIS Learning Rep could work together to promote CPD in the area'.

The LRs were asked if they had a good working relationship with their LA CPD QIO prior to the event being organised. There was a fifty-fifty split in the answers and the following answer is indicative of the barriers encountered by some of the LRs:

'While I had met with the Support for Staff Service Manager on several occasions, she was not prepared to work with me it appeared. I suggested that it might be useful to involve me in the CPD Reference Group & she made all sorts of excuses for this not to happen'.

The LRs were then asked if their working relationship with the officers had improved or developed since the event. The answers were more positive with four stating that the relationship had improved and developed whilst two stated that it had not. One LR gave the following explanation as to why this was the case:

'However, although still not involved in CPD Reference Group, has allowed me, after my suggestions to come and speak to the CPD Coordinators (Sec.) Meeting regarding my role. Reminded me that some CPD Coordinators not keen on me coming to their meeting, as I only represented one union. Agrees to meet with me occasionally, always very busy, doesn't see our working together as necessary or important'.

Although this may be an isolated case, it should be a cause for concern because if this is being repeated in a number of authorities it firstly, undermines the partnership approach based on the *21st Century Agreement* and as currently advocated by the Scottish Government (2007) and secondly, the LRs and their ability to carry out their role and responsibilities effectively and efficiently.

The following examples are indicative of positive effects and outcomes of such events:

'Wider networking opportunity. Staff pressing H.Teacher to have us visit. Lifting of self-esteem of teachers making them motivated to do it for themselves'.

'It has increased my profile within the authority and in some schools. It has helped, personally, in my ability to communicate and work with council officials/outside agencies effectively. It also enhanced my understanding of the standards required to become a CT'.

As for the impact these events have had on the LRs themselves, the respondents were positive as the following examples indicate:

'I am now organising the Providers' Open afternoon (also an event previously done by [local authority] *CPD manager). I will be organising the next joint Spring conference and my personal client list has expanded and several colleagues are now doing Module 1. I am enjoying the work and it is heartening to know that it is a contribution to the CPD process for colleagues. Having backing of CPD Manager gets us into schools'.*

'Recognition by colleagues where I work and teachers from other schools in the L.A. at CPD events. I know this as I am often informally asked for advice – My disappointment in the system is that I very rarely have been asked for a formal appointment – teachers presently do not seem to want to take that step further for advice in their career'.

The LRs were asked if their profile had been raised amongst teachers in their authority area due to the CPD event. In all six cases they stated it had but one of the respondents tempered their positive response with the following additional comment: *'...but still little personal contact from members'.*

In terms of how successful the CPD events had been the respondents made the following observations:

'We had over 60 people attend and I know of 6 colleagues who are doing Module 1 as a result. [The local authority] *CPD manager wants it to be an annual event. Our* [local association] *EIS Executive supports us fully in this project and with pay for the breakfast at the conference'.*

'All three have been successful in their own way – possibly the 1st and

3rd more so. Each year numbers have increased and an evaluation carried out at the last event resulted in very positive feedback'.

All six respondents stated that there were plans to hold joint events in their area in the future although one of them tempered their response with the following proviso:

'...but not at present due to the uncertainty in who will be the contact person and all the new school builds we feel that staff will want to concentrate on this'.

The LRs responded to the invitation to make additional comments in relation to the issues raised by the questionnaire and their answers. The following observations should help the EIS and other stakeholders construct a meaningful strategy in terms of reaching teachers in relation to CPD and CT:

'I thought that the event would encourage school reps to invite me in to talk to the staff in connection with the CT route and other CPD issues, to explain what I could do for the whole staff or individual. I did send out a flyer to every school through the local association mailing but still little contact, (will try to send out a further flyer this year'.

'Despite it being around since 2000, the idea of teachers having "to do" [CPD] (as part of their job remit) is still seen as a chore. Many teachers are still finding the prospect of being learners daunting and therefore do not take full advantage of engaging in CPD unless prompted to do so by HT or line manager. This takes away ownership from the individual and also having someone else drive their CPD teachers do not feel the need for advice on how to take forward their own development/ career. In turn this results in EIS Learning Reps finding progress slow especially in offering formal support to their members'.

One of the respondents who completed a personal record wrote about a CPD event she was organising and what she hoped it would achieve from a number of perspectives. Her observations overlap with issues raised in the evidence presented above and show what a difficult position LRs find themselves in with their local authorities and colleagues:

'My own "institution" is an IT support unit for schools (still seconded). I must admit I haven't said a lot about the LR role although they all know I do it. I think they've been a bit unclear about it. Anyway, as we're planning a big CPD event soon I've asked them if they'd like a stand – because we are a major provider of CPD anyway. It's also a chance for

each section of the team to explain a bit more about what we do. We've been working on a presentation along these lines anyway. I think this will help them see what it is I do on Thu PM [Thursday afternoon]. *I'll be on the EIS stand, and will be contributing to the event'* (Personal Record 5).

Lyn McClintock has been instrumental in getting the CPD events initiative off the ground and in her opinion there was a specific need for these events as she explains:

'I thought that if teachers saw that the authorities and the union were working together to promote CPD it would have several benefits: it would promote CPD generally, improve relations between authorities and the union and bring requests for assistance from members for the LRs' (McClintock, 2007: 3).

To date, CPD events have been held in South Lanarkshire, Perth and Kinross, Dumfries and Galloway, Fife, Clackmannanshire, West Dunbartonshire and Edinburgh authorities. I have attended some of these and they have been an undoubted success on many fronts as stakeholders have banded together to ensure this. The LRs and CPD QIOs have got together to organise and promote the events; CPD and CT providers have pitched up with and manned stalls and a number of respected individuals have given keynote presentations including representatives from the GTCS, HMIE and eminent academics as well as the LRs and officers themselves. The EIS LR Administrator highlighted the following example as to the success of these events:

'It was felt that a maximum of 60 teachers would attend and 45 actually attended the event...The venue was excellent and may well have played a part in ensuring attendance. It was held from 4pm so there was no issue of time off for people to attend – it was open to all teachers, not just EIS MEMBERS. The most interesting thing was that after the event finished there was a line of people waiting to speak to the two speakers and [the LR]. *The following day 12 people signed up for CT and* [the LR] *has had more contact and an invitation to attend a meeting of school members. From the success of this event it was felt that it was feasible to try and roll these out across Scotland'* (McClintock, 2007: 3-4).

Discussions are currently in progress regarding further joint events in other local authorities throughout Scotland.

Partnership Working Between School-Based LRs and LA CPD QIOs

In relation to School LRs the situation is significantly different and far more negative. Fourteen (70%) indicated that they were not working in partnership with LA CPD QIOs, whilst less than a third (6) stated that they were. Of those that were, the following examples are indicative of the nature of their partnership working:

'Indirectly through Multi-Establishment LRs...One meeting – attended to be aware of LA CPD structure...Contact via email and occasional meeting...But through IT developments/blogging'.

Of the participants who answered in the negative, one expanded upon their answer as follows:

'No, but keep in contact with Multi-Establishment LR'.

From the above answers it seems obvious that the main relationship at local authority level is between the CPD QIOs and the ME LRs and it is fair to state this should be the case but it may be worthwhile for the LA CPD QIOs to make themselves known to the School LRs and have the occasional meeting to ensure that lines of communication are kept open. As the next sub-section will show, the key relationship for the School LRs is with their respective School CPD Co-ordinators.

Partnership Working With School CPD Co-ordinators

The LRs were asked if they worked in partnership with School CPD Co-ordinators and the answers make for interesting reading as they are far more positive in relation to the School LRs. Of the ME LRs five (41.7%) stated that they were working in partnership with the Co-ordinators whilst seven (58.3%) indicated they were not. The ME LRs who answered in the affirmative described the nature of their partnership working as follows:

'CPD Authority Meetings...Amicable co-existence – not really working with, most work at authority level. Am based in school but work peripatetically...In the absence of School L-Reps I may be asked to liaise with CPD Co-ordinators...I am a member of the CPD Coordinators Committee...I am the School CPD Adviser!'

One of the participants who stated they were not working in partnership with the Co-ordinators seemed to be suggesting they had an informal partnership with them as the following statement indicates:

'We were invited to their last conference last June. I've emailed them all about promoting the first CT network meeting – and it certainly increased the members attending. Will also involve them in publicising May event. There was talk of our attending any CPD aimed at them – so far just the conference. Though we were also invited to a CPD organisers meeting, which I attended and found very informative'.

As indicated above the situation in relation to School LRs and their relationship with their School counterparts seems to be far more positive. Eleven (55%) stated they were working in partnership with their School CPD Co-ordinators whilst nine (45%) stated they were not. Of those that were, the following examples are indicative of the nature of their partnership working:

'Already CPD Co-ordinator...Membership of school's CPD group headed by Depute Rector – plans school CPD programme...Loosely – am/have been given autonomy to lead a learning team to provide support/training opportunities in school'.

'I am School CPD Coordinator...At times we meet to discuss the learning opportunities available to colleagues and how we can widen these – no timetabled meeting though...I work closely with Senior Depute with responsibility for CPD issues. I have delivered CPD talk to all staff in conjunction...I am liaising with the School's CPD Co-ordinator to review the planning and dissemination of whole-school opportunities'.

Of those who were not working in partnership, one participant explained why this was the case as follows:

'Arriving at this school on secondment, I introduced myself as LR but the member of BOM responsible for CPD arrangements has continued to do this without my contribution'.

Four of the respondents who completed personal records expanded on this issue as follows:

'Have informal experience at Local Authority CPD courses (though I would hope to make formal partnership if [I become] *Multi-Establishment LR'* (This respondent is currently a School LR) (Personal Record 2).

We haven't done any joint working with CPD coordinators but do get invited to their annual conference. We also get invited to meetings for CPD course providers, so we're kept well informed' (Personal Record 5).

'My local authority has supported the role and I work in collaboration with the authority's CPD manager. I have been introduced to all school CPD Advisors although I feel I have to work hard with most of them to remind them of my existence. However, the ones who have taken my role on board, consult me regularly when a member of staff needs CPD advice/support/information. They also pass on my name to other CPD Coordinators who need advice for colleagues' (Personal Record 6).

'Mixed...some cooperation, but generally left out of the loop when relevant matters are being considered...v. limited partnership working (The union consider they have the more able people and can win arguments! Lots of policies and agreements are written by the union side. To what extent are the Authority aware that they benefit from this? I doubt they are conscious of it – but who knows)...I think our Head Teacher is the CPD co-ordinator for the school' (Personal Record 6).

The above evidence has highlighted a factor that could be a potential concern in that some of the School LRs are also School CPD Co-ordinators. This raises the issue of a conflict of interest and the question, should a person be undertaking both roles simultaneously?

Learning Representatives Being Co-opted on to CPD Related Working Groups and Committees

The participants were asked if they had been co-opted on to CPD related working groups or committees and in the case of the ME LRs the answers are encouraging but not so for the School LRs. Eight (66.7%) of ME LRs stated they had been co-opted whilst five (33.3%) stated they had not. Of the participants who answered in the affirmative they described the type of groups and committees they sit on as follows:

'LA CPD Management Group, Chartered Teachers' Network, Supply Teachers' Steering Group, RICCT Teachers' Steering Group...CPD Ad Hoc Committee...G.L.O.W. - CPD/PRD Policy Committee – Council Learning agreement Working Group...CPD Coordinators Group. CPD Steering Group'.

The following comment was made by one of the LRs who had also given a positive answer:

'I have volunteered to be a GLOW mentor and to take part in GLOW activities but heard nothing. I have contacted Council CPD organisers but

have had no replies. On a plus note I have been asked to attend the Health and Safety Liaison Group meetings but so far have been unable to attend as my head teacher could not let me go at that time due to staff illness'.

The LRs who responded in the negative explained why this was the case as follows:

'Consequences of present status as outlined in other responses' [This LR does not have a formal time-off agreement and has minimal funded cover]...*Local Authority anti-trade union. Don't know if they have them! In the dark!'*

As stated above the situation in relation to the School LRs being co-opted on to groups and committees is not so positive. Only six (30%) stated they had been co-opted whilst fourteen stated they had not. The participants who answered in the affirmative described the working groups and committees they sit on as follows:

'Cluster CPD Group to help organise cluster CPD events...Whole school CPD working group...Already have core CPD role in school... Excel developments in [local authority area]...*A Curriculum for Excellence...Language Working Party for the authority'. Chartered Teacher Network meetings'...Review Group to formulate/simply CPD information/dissemination policy'.*

The LRs that gave a negative answer explained why this is the case as follows:

'Nobody is interested. We have a multi-establishment LR but I am the only establishment-based LR in the region. My previous school considered that "only schools without a good CPD co-ordinator" would need one anyway (not that their's was a fair system!) and I am on a secondment post here... The opportunity hasn't arisen. CPD working groups are more prevalent in the secondary sector. CPD coordination in primary schools is usually the responsibility of one individual... There are none...I am unaware of any in the area...L Reps not seen as important resource'.

'We are a very small school – if anyone needs advice they ask me. – Appropriate CPD for our school is more of a problem – IT COSTS A LOT!'

It is clear from the evidence presented that in terms of the LRs becoming embedded within their local authority CPD structures there is still work to do in terms of being members of specific CPD working groups and committees. LA CPD QIOs should as a matter of importance look as to how they can integrate LRs onto such working bodies. It is clear from the evidence presented thus far that EIS LRs have much to offer operational stakeholders and are more than willing to work in partnership with both the QIOs and Co-ordinators to further the professional development agenda pertaining to teachers.

The next chapter will examine the relationship between the LRs and their colleagues.

8

Learning Representatives Connecting with Colleagues

Introduction

This chapter will examine whether the positive working relationship built up between the LRs and their local authority and school counterparts is having a knock-on effect in terms of the LRs being able to connect with their colleagues. It is paramount to the long-term sustainability of this initiative, as the first study highlighted relatively few teachers taking up the opportunity to seek advice, guidance and support from the EIS LRs. A factor also highlighted by Douglas Cairns of the HMIE in a previous chapter.

Colleagues Seeking Advice and Guidance from the Learning Representatives

The participants were asked if colleagues regularly asked them for advice and guidance and the answers make for grim reading. Only four ME LRs (33.3%) answered in the affirmative and eight (66.7%) stated they were not regularly contacted by their colleagues for advice and guidance. Asked why this was the case they gave the following answers:

'As I am not formally promoting my role I'm not asked for regular advice. I have spoken to colleagues who know I am a learning rep…No agreed time-off. Not really started Multi-Establishment work – But have worked with colleagues in own schools (I think productively) and introduced self to a few staff from other schools)….This has been v. slow to build. People wary of union activity. Have outdated idea of union even though members; Most people only beginning to get to grips with CPD etc and LA has a comprehensive service…Not enough awareness raising nationally. I get no facility time or real recognition from Local Authority so difficult for me to drum up business!...I don't know. I am asked about other work-related matters. Perhaps I have too many offices

for them to home in on the LR one. The few who do ask for advice do come back for more. I think they appreciate that the advice is well founded and sound....It's building up, but I probably wouldn't say its regular yet. A lot of people know I'm a CT and CT advisor and ask me for advice anyway, without realising I'm a LR as well...I have no idea I'm afraid. Presumably they don't feel the need... Colleagues have asked for advice & guidance, but this is slow at the moment. Working to raise my profile'.

Interestingly, the situation is somewhat more positive amongst the School LRs. Eight (40%) indicated that colleagues regularly sought advice and guidance from them, whilst eleven (55%) stated their colleagues did not and one participant (5%) did not answer the question. The following explanations are examples from the LRs who indicated that their colleagues did not regularly seek advice and guidance from them:

'I have given advice and guidance when asked and this has been fruitful but not at all regular... Occasionally but not always able to help due to management still controlling CPD...In my last school a small number would approach me but CPD a v. low priority...Most people autonomously select course/reading relevant to own need...Few know that I am an LR, and we have no time for dialogue...Ask in my role as CPD Coordinator, rather than LR... Colleagues (establishment) largely self-motivated. Occasional advice, not regular...I have had only one colleague approach myself... I do publicise courses and try and connect electronically... Some colleagues ask advice in Chartered Teacher work as they know I have my Masters otherwise no'.

Four of the respondents who completed personal records dealt with this issue and overall, their observations were consistent with the above comments in terms of their negative overtones.

The non-connection with members as highlighted by these negative answers can in part be linked to a lack of experience, in that ten out of the above twelve respondents who answered in the negative or gave no answer have not held a union position before. In part the lack of colleagues coming through the door to seek advice and guidance can be put down to inexperience in the role as a union activist. Holinrake et al. (2008: 400) point out that the findings of their study '...suggests that many newly trained ULRs find their first attempts to develop workplace learning to be a daunting and isolating experience'. It also highlights the need for the EIS to do more at both national and local level to raise awareness of the existence of LRs and ensure that they have assistance both from local activists and national and area officials in promoting their role.

The inability of the LRs to connect with members is an ongoing problem. To ascertain why this is the case I decided to carry out a short one-to-one questionnaire survey amongst teachers who were attending one of the CPD events jointly organised by LRs and LA CPD QIOs in 2007. It was estimated that anywhere between thirty to fifty teachers would attend and I decided that I would attempt to survey thirty participants. On the day forty four teachers turned up and thirty were approached to participate in the survey. All thirty agreed to be involved in this part of the research process. The results make for interesting reading and shed further light as to why teachers are not engaging with the LRs in significant numbers.

Of the thirty participants, twenty four (80%) were EIS members, so in theory they should have all known about the Institute's LRs to some degree. However, as the following findings will indicate this is far from being the case. The participants were asked if they read the Institute's regularly published members' magazine, the Scottish Educational Journal (SEJ). The reason they were asked this question is because the SEJ regularly runs features on the LRs and their activities and at the back of each edition there is information and contact details for the LRs. Nineteen (63.3%) stated they did read the SEJ article whilst eleven (36.7%) admitted they did not. This snapshot indicates that a number of EIS members are not getting the message that there are representatives who can help advise and guide them in relation to CPD and CT.

The EIS may have to examine ways in which it can make the SEJ more attractive to read, particularly when there are so many other competing interests for the precious free time of teachers and as the following explanation from Lyn McClintock runs counter to the evidence above:

'One of the issues which was highlighted in the first evaluation and has been discussed widely at LR meetings is that there is still not as much contact from members for the LRs as we had hoped. We have established a campaign of constant publicity for the LRs. As well as the contact details for multi LRs featuring in every edition of the SEJ, each SEJ also contains articles on CPD, CT and LRs. Individual LRs have

written articles about why they became an LR, what they were doing etc. We think that members relate to seeing something in the SEJ by someone from their particular area or school. Articles about CPD and CT also keep this to the forefront and constantly remind members how important and beneficial CPD is. The next thing we are planning to do is to get teachers who have been helped by LRs quoted in the SEJ. This is the next logical step and will help to personalise LRs and what they can do for members' (McClintock, 2007: 3).

The participants were then asked if they knew what a LR is and sixteen (53.3%) admitted they did not know what a LR is while fourteen (46.7%) did. This is despite the fact that four-fifths of the participants were EIS members. Again this suggests that at both local and national level the EIS is failing to get the message across to its members that LRs exist and are there to help and guide members in relation to CPD and CT.

The participants were asked if they had utilised the services of a LR and unsurprisingly the overwhelming majority had not. In fact only two (6.7%) had. The participants who answered in the affirmative were asked if it had been a positive experience and both indicated it had been and described how as follows:

'Very helpful because I am going through Chartered Teacher... The Learning Representative is knowledgeable, approachable and professional'.

These positive experiences indicate there is a chink of light for the EIS and its LRs. If the Institute can build upon the good work that the LRs are carrying out (albeit on a limited scale) and publicise it at both local and national level using as many communication mediums as are available this may well stimulate more interest amongst the membership and encourage teachers to seek out the LRs for advice and guidance.

The participants who stated they had not utilised the services of LRs were asked why this was the case and the following diverse examples give an indication as to why this is the case:

'I am not in a mainstream school setting because most of my work is social work orientated...I've only been teaching three months...I have not felt the need to...It was only after I had completed Chartered Teacher that I got to know that they existed...I did not know they existed until I looked on the [EIS] *website...Time – Reflective Time – Shortage of*

it...If I do not know what one is how can I utilise one?...I have not
needed their assistance...Not aware how they could help me...I did not
know how to access them but since attending this event I now know there
is a Thursday drop-in session which I will attend at some point...Because
we have a CPD Co-ordinator in school and she makes our life easier'.

The above comments indicate a significant core of EIS members is unaware of the existence of LRs and what they can do for them. However, as one of the above comments shows, if the members are alerted to the existence of the LRs then they will be willing to utilise their services as and when it is appropriate to them and their CPD requirements.

The Institute should note the above findings and the challenge the Scottish Government has laid down to trade unions in terms of developing the position of LRs within their organisations. The evidence suggests this is not happening, particularly at local level. The EIS may have to consider strongly advising local associations to put together a strategy to inform members within their local authority area as to the existence, role and responsibilities of EIS LRs.

One approach could be for local association lay officers and activists along with ME and School LRs to visit each and every school in their designated area and inform teachers that the LRs are there to help them. If they adopt this approach they may want to show a short film about professional development and LRs in Scotland, screened on Teachers' TV in February 2008. It features two LRs talking about their activities, role and their own CPD and Dr Jim O'Brien of the University of Edinburgh discussing various issues pertaining to the professional development agenda in Scottish education (Teachers' TV, 2008).

A second could be to use a new ICT tool that has been created by the Trades Union Congress (TUC) and adopted by the STUC. It is called the *union learning Climbing Frame*. As the TUC (2007) explains:

'The union learning Climbing Frame is an easy-to-use electronic tool which allows learning reps to create pathways of learning and action plans for individuals that can be reviewed and updated as they progress on their learning journey.

It also provides up-to-date information and advice for ULRs about a broad range of learning opportunities, and also allows individual unions to adapt it to their own needs.

In addition, ULRs can keep ongoing records of who they're working with and where they're heading, while unions can generate accurate profiles of their own learners.

It is set to make life a lot easier for ULRs and is certain to help promote the idea of learning in the workplace'.

A third approach should be to organise joint CPD events as the evidence above shows they are a proactive method of informing teachers that LRs exist as well as explaining to them what LRs do and how they can help them.

Lyn McClintock has highlighted a fourth approach and that is for there to be a significant EIS LRs presence at the Scottish Learning Festival. In the past two years the LRs have conducted well attended seminars at the festival and she describes the positive impact of this initiative as follows:

'... There were around 20 people at each seminar which is a good number for these types of seminar and the Mentoring and Coaching seminar caused considerable discussion. Both seminars gave the LRs the opportunity to promote themselves and what they can do to assist teachers. Having attended all the seminars to date I felt a change in the ones this year – with larger audiences and the fact that those present were asking questions of the LRs. I feel that their role is becoming more widely known. I also feel that respect for our LRs is growing' LRs' (McClintock, 2007: 6-7).

The LRs have also made their presence felt at the Scottish Parliament by participating in what was termed "Trade Union Week", where they met up with MSPs and spoke about their experiences, achievements and the problems they faced (McClintock, 2007: 6-7).

The final part of the chapter will analyse how the LRs interact with colleagues and how effective the interaction has been.

Types of Interaction the Learning Representatives have with Colleagues

The participants were given a series of options in relation to describing the type of activities they organised in order to liaise with their colleagues. The respondents were allowed to choose more than one option. The ME LRs gave the following answers: six organised meetings with colleagues; seven organised dedicated one-to-one sessions with colleagues; two had meetings with School CPD Co-ordinators; eight had meetings with LA CPD QIOs; three had meetings with head teachers; four organised CPD Open Days; one had created a dedicated website. Five had engaged in other activities as the following examples show:

'I regularly speak at CPD open evenings for University of Edinburgh. Involved in setting up a Chartered Teacher network in my region...I run meetings with interest networks...CT Open Day...Set up Joint Union/Authority CPD Event'.

One respondent who took up the opportunity to explain how they planned to engage with members as follows:

'...I am hoping to target teachers in years 2-6 (those not eligible for c teach yet) as I feel this could be a captive market. I'm hoping to promote the GTC Professional Recognition Prog as a stepping stone into management or c teach'.

In relation to School LRs they gave the following answers: eleven had organised meetings with colleagues; nine had organised one-to-one sessions with colleagues; six had meetings with School CPD Co-ordinators; only one had meetings with LA CPD QIOs; four had meetings with their head master; and not none participant had either organised a CPD Open Day or set up a dedicated website. Four participants indicated that they had engaged in other activities as the following examples show:

'Setting up a learning team in response to whole-school developmental need...Have raised awareness of role at School EIS meeting and passed on info...Blog created for Chartered Teachers'.

The last example is an interesting development and again shows how the EIS LRs are willing to use IT to aid them in their role.

Of particular concern to stakeholders should be the answer given by one of the participants who could not answer the question at all and gave the following explanation as to why they could not even organise meetings with their colleagues:

'Attempted this – not permitted'.

Four of the respondents who completed personal records dealt with this subject and their observations add to and expand on the evidence above as the following comments indicate:

'To further the role of the LR I have used lists of members that I acquired through my position on the Local Association Executive and have attempted direct contact... [with members] ...through our First Class email system. I send details of courses and events and report on meetings. Not everyone is on First Class but I reach a large number of people that way' (Personal Record 1).

'CPD feedback forms for teachers and facilitating ways of passing on their information/experiences to [the] Department/whole –school colleagues. Twilight courses in school' (Personal Record 2).

'The local authority has been fine. Before the time out was agreed we started having regular meetings with CPD. We've set up a charter teacher network with them and have had a big CT event. Now we're working together on a CPD event. We're always welcome to add to the CPD bulletins and updates' (Personal Record 5).

'I try to focus on raising awareness of the role within the authority whenever an opportunity presents itself – by starting and supporting informal networking groups, by promoting any successful CPD achievements that have been influenced by the L Rep and by joining in with initiatives suggested by the CPD Advisor' (Personal Record 6).

Karen Gilmore stated that since the first study changes had been made to the LR training courses to ensure they are more practically orientated and new LRs are better equipped to interact with their colleagues. Karen explained that the undergraduate module is very practical in nature and the assignment is a piece of action research. The action research is about creating a toolkit for LRs to use when liaising with colleagues. The undergraduate course helps the student LRs to develop in terms of ensuring they have the skills to allow them to deliver as LRs in a practical and progressive manner on behalf of their colleagues (Gilmore, 2007).

Karen pointed out the students are carrying out the action research project to produce the following:

- Learning styles inventory;
- Training needs analysis;
- A directory of resources which teachers can access, which in turn the LRs are encouraged to adapt and add to after they have been accredited;
- A training evaluation tool for their colleagues. This is so teachers can feedback to the LRs as to the merits and demerits of

the courses they have attended. This is beneficial to both teachers and the LRs.

All of the above are piloted on two colleagues who then evaluate the LR on their performance and quality of the tools and the LRs then write-up a narrative of their colleagues' responses. This approach is all about the potential LRs having a go at being a LR before they are accredited and helps Karen observe how they are developing (Gilmore, 2007).

Karen also highlighted one more significant change to the courses and this is project work. She gives the prospective LRs projects that will help them develop future resources as follows:

• The ME students are asked to analyse a new initiative to ensure that they have a sound knowledge of what it is and further ensures the practical nature of the course;

• Single establishment students are asked to undertake group project work. They are asked to analyse initiatives in their own and the Further Education sector as follows - describe what it is; outline the opportunities and limitations for CPD and the implications for the role of LRs.

The aim of this approach is to encourage the LRs to undertake projects that will be relevant to their future role and responsibilities as a LR and give them a fundamental understanding of CPD and CT from the strategic stakeholders' perspective. Another change that has been implemented through the *Blackboard* technology is that an experienced LR will answer student LRs questions in a type of '...*ask the expert exercise'* (Gilmore, 2007).

To test how well LRs are interacting with colleagues, a small number of teachers from two local authorities who had sought advice and guidance from LRs were asked to give an account of their experiences. The teachers were EIS members and had between 5-30 years service. The participants teach a variety of subjects and perform different roles. One of the teachers was aware of the existence of LRs from their inception, whilst two became aware of LRs once their colleague became an accredited LR about two years ago and one of the teachers became aware of the existence of LRs in the past year.

The participants were asked to explain what they understood to be the role of EIS LRs and they gave the following answers:

'To make teachers aware of the professional development opportunities available' (Teacher 1 Interview).

'To facilitate the members accessing information, advice and consultation on professional development and they are separate from what the authority provides in relation to CPD advice and guidance' (Teacher 2 Interview).

'Facilitator with the school to help teachers find out about funding and courses for CPD as well as providing ongoing advice and guidance on CPD matters' (Teacher 3 Interview).

'To increase teachers' personal and professional learning and advising and guiding teachers on CPD courses and whether funding is available to them' (Teacher 4 Interview).

These answers show the participants have a clear understanding as to the general role of EIS LRs. The participants were asked what their initial contact was with a LR. In all four cases contact was made because they knew their respective LRs and were in close working proximity to them. This is positive on one level as the LRs have made an impact on their immediate work colleagues but may mean that they have much work to do to reach colleagues in other schools within their authority areas be they ME or School LRs. However, one of the participants explained that initial contact came about because the LR e-mailed all the teachers in the authority informing them that he was an accredited LR (Teacher 4 Interview).

The teachers were asked why they made contact with the LRs and they gave the following answers:

'When I realised I could get professional recognition from the GTC for the work I was doing in primary schools in relation to literacy' (Teacher 1 Interview).

This participant went on to explain that she did not actually approach the LR it was the LR who approached her and stated that she take the above mentioned route. This teacher tellingly stated *'...so that is a learning representative doing their job'*.

Another participant explained she is a CPD Co-ordinator, a role she shares with another colleague. She went on to explain that the LR keeps her abreast of developments and in turn the Co-ordinator asks the LR to participate in some in-service training days in terms of explaining to teachers the role of the LR (Teacher 2 Interview).

The two other participants explained their contact with a LR as follows:

'In this school it's hard not to make contact with the LR and when I started the Chartered Teacher course that was the formal way but informally [the LR] *will come with articles or something off a website that might be useful to a teacher for their own subject or CPD course they are on'* (Teacher 3 Interview).

'Because he was in the staff room, he was available and he is enthusiastic about encouraging teachers to undertake courses' (Teacher 4 Interview).

The teachers were asked what type of assistance they had been given by the LRs and they answered as follows:

'How to fill in the GTC forms but there seems to be a vagueness by the GTC as how best to fill in these forms and the LR helped me get through the vagueness of the filling in of the forms, for example what to put in each section' (Teacher 1 Interview).

'…some teachers have asked me for advice about Chartered Teacher and I have passed them on to the LR' (Teacher 2 Interview).

'He gave us books and articles he used; booklists; some of his own work because he had completed Chartered Teacher himself and he explained how he had done the Chartered Teacher course although he had done it online and I am doing it through UHI/University of Strathclyde. He also commented on which books he felt were worthwhile. He was a good starting point for the literature review' (Teacher 3 Interview).

'I went to him about Chartered Teacher and not only did he encourage me to undertake Chartered Teacher and which provider to go to, he has also continued to ask how I am doing and encouraging me to stick with it. He is very prepared to discuss every aspect of what you are doing in CPD terms which is good. He also has a significant collection of books which he lends us to help us with our studies' (Teacher Interview 4).

The above comments show the LRs the participants have been in contact with are committed, enthusiastic, knowledgeable and in one case a clear role model. This is an important finding as in a previous section of this evaluation LA CPD QIOs made it clear that if LRs were to have a long-term future and be a key point of contact for their colleagues they had to be regarded as role models. The evidence suggests that there is at least one such LR and the likelihood is that there are many others in the same mould.

The teachers were asked how they had used and do use the advice and guidance of the LRs and they gave the following answers:

'... *The LR told me to meet with my line manager in relation to this exercise* [the filling in of the GTCS forms for Professional Recognition] *as there is a section in the form that needs to be filled in by the line manager to support the application*' (Teacher 1 Interview).

'...*gives you an awareness of what to do and the pitfalls of undertaking such* [CT] *courses. He has been useful in relaying his experience of doing Chartered Teacher through a different provider and this was a good comparison to use. Also for the accreditation for the APL for Chartered Teacher,* [the LR] *has been very good and he has gone through the process and has helped me with useful advice and guidance in relation to my own APL application*' (Teacher 3 Interview).

'*Use it to motivate myself and bounce ideas off him and he is prepared to do this*' (Teacher 4 Interview).

The second and third observations are further proof that a LR can be a positive role model for their colleagues and this will help in persuading even the most cynical and hard-bitten teachers there are professional development opportunities that will be of practical use to them.

Taking this point one step further, the participants were asked what impact the advice, guidance and support they had received from the LRs has had on them from a professional and or classroom perspective. They gave the following explanations:

'*I now have GTC recognition for literacy and supporting pupil learning and with the advice and guidance of the LR it now means that I can go and look for jobs in other local authorities. It gives me a bit of an edge when applying for jobs*' (Teacher 1 Interview).

'*For me as a manager it has been very useful having someone as knowledgeable as the LR which I can access . It has been very good for me as the LR feeds back information on CPD courses and new initiatives that are coming up that have a professional development perspective*' (Teacher 2 Interview).

'*Very useful, particularly considering size* [of this small] *school and where there has not been a history of CPD amongst staff, particularly as a lot of senior teachers have not undertaken significant CPD since they left teacher training college. With* [the LR] *here, you can chew the fat with him about which CPD courses to undertake and his advice and guidance is invaluable because we do not have the same breadth of network of other teachers and schools in relation to dealing with CPD. [The LR] is proactive and acts as a catalyst to promote CPD amongst all staff'* (Teacher 3 Interview).

'In this school because we are so small he encourages us to maintain a focus that such CPD is about maintaining standards for the whole of Scottish education. He makes us look at the bigger picture in education terms. He actually confronts all of us including senior management to think about CPD and related issue' (Teacher 4 Interview).

The above comments illustrate the LRs in these two authorities are having a positive impact on the colleagues they have assisted. Not only in terms of helping them progress their careers and pursue CT but also to think about and acknowledge that their CPD will and should have a positive impact on those that matter most – the pupils they teach.

The relationship between these teachers and the LRs they have assisted has not stopped with the initial advice, guidance and support as all four teachers stated they continue to have ongoing and regular contact with these LRs, because they work in close proximity and have become engaged in a CPD discourse with them. This can be regarded as a significant and positive move forward, as the LRs are actively promoting professional development; acting as role models and engaging colleagues in discussions that keeps the issue of CPD on the agenda of both schools and teachers.

This has had a further positive impact on one of the participants, as they are now discussing with the LR which training options she should consider for her present position and her future aspirations (Teacher 1 Interview).

The teachers were asked if they could differentiate between the roles of CPD Co-ordinators and LRs and they gave the following answers:

'CPD Co-ordinators are usually based within a department or school and the LR is usually authority-based' (Teacher 1 Interview).

'The LR has in-depth knowledge of CPD courses and initiatives that goes beyond that of CPD Co-ordinators. Thus is able to give impartial and valued advice to both me, my team and teachers' (Teacher 2 Interview).

'In my experience CPD Co-ordinators just organise the courses while [the LR] promotes the learning and the advice and guidance. The CPD

Co-ordinators organise courses at strategic level while [the LR] *is more hands-on at the operational level and provides more incentive for teachers to actively participate in CPD and Chartered Teacher courses because he comes with information on these courses and informs and supports you on them whilst the CPD Co-ordinators do this'* (Teacher 3 Interview).

'The CPD Co-ordinator as far as I understand creates our in-service programmes and sends out by e-mail what CPD courses are currently available in the [authority area]. *[The LR] is more personable, he encourages you to do CPD courses rather than just informing you about them'* (Teacher 4 Interview).

These explanations show teachers see a clear and definite differentiation in the roles of LRs and CPD Co-ordinators. The evidence also suggests the LRs are regarded as motivators and persuaders in terms of teachers being actively encouraged to pursue some form of professional development.

The participants were asked if they felt the LRs had made an impact at both authority and school level. In three cases they could not, whilst one participant made the following observation:

'The LR has made a big impact on the Authority as she sits on a number of strategic working groups and committees. For example, she sits on the Curriculum for Excellence Working Group and that is testament itself to how important she is to Authority in terms of professional development of teachers in this Authority' (Teacher 2 Interview).

The participants were asked how they thought LRs could improve their colleagues' understanding of CPD and the benefits of CPD. Not all the participants had a view on this issue but those who did made the following observations:

'Sometimes teachers think CPD is just about attending courses but the LR can widen their horizons by showing that professional development is much wider in terms of what they can undertake and achieve' (Teacher 2 Interview).

'...because LRs are up-to-date on the courses which are available and can pass on this information to teachers as well as being able to give advice and guidance on funding opportunities to take up these courses' (Teacher 3 Interview).

'CPD does not just have to be focussed on the narrow view that comes out of the Authority. The Authority does not encourage teachers to do Chartered Teacher and how such CPD will help you in the classroom.

[The LR] *does believe in Chartered Teacher and promotes the benefit of it in terms of confidence in teachers being able to express their opinions which teachers have lost over the years and teachers should be autonomous and confident in expressing their views'* (Teacher 4 Interview).

These observations show teachers who have been in contact with LRs and have benefited from their advice, guidance and support see a long-term future for LRs in promoting the benefits of professional development. Particularly, from the perspectives of improving classroom practice, increasing teachers' confidence and giving teachers the ability to challenge the orthodox thinking of their employers and senior management (also highlighted by Reeves, 2007). If this is achieved in a constructive manner, it can only serve to improve teaching standards for the benefit of pupils and the Scottish education system.

Based on their own observations the participants were asked how they thought the profile of LRs could be raised in their authority areas. Two of the teachers did not have a view, whilst another stated if she had not been working alongside the LR, she would have been unaware of the LR and her colleagues in other authorities were unaware of LRs. This participant went on to state that she was unaware of how LRs were structured within each local authority (Teacher 1 Interview). However, one of the teachers had a definite view on this issue which is concordant with the views expressed by some of the LA CPD QIOs. The teacher stated that:

'LRs would and should be used as facilitators and mentors in relation to certain professional development initiatives' (Teacher 2 Interview).

The teachers were asked if they would consider becoming LRs and in all four cases they were emphatic that they did not want to become one. Two of the participants explained why and they gave the following similar answers:

'No, I have enough on my plate' (Teacher 3 Interview).

'Not right now, I have a big enough workload as it is' (Teacher 4 Interview).

If nothing else these comments show how committed an individual must be to take on the role of a LR because they too must have a significant teaching workload as well as other family and outside commitments.

Two of the participants made additional comments as follows:

'*The LR initiative is a good initiative, it needs to be built upon and it must become sustainable*' (Teacher 2 Interview).

'*Funding of CPD courses is an issue. A good aspect of* [the LR] *is that you feel you can go to him for advice and guidance and will be well received and get some constructive advice and guidance. He is well respected within the school and within the local authority area*' (Teacher 3 Interview).

These comments show how embedded these particular LRs have become within their respective authority areas and in one case they are clearly well respected and regarded as a role model for teachers and school management alike.

The next chapter will examine further difficulties the participants have faced as well as looking to the future.

9

Obstacles and Prospects for the Learning Representatives

Introduction

This chapter will deal with the obstacles and problems the second main cohort of LRs has encountered to date in relation to their role and responsibilities. It will also analyse what effect being a LR has had on this cohort and what the future holds for these LRs.

Additional Obstacles and Problems Highlighted by Learning Representatives

A number of the respondents who completed personal records highlighted further obstacles and problems they felt would hinder them in the future in terms of effectively and efficiently discharging their role and responsibilities as LRs as the following indicative observations highlight:

'In all, I have been very lucky to have had a 'problem free' journey in my LR role. One potential problem I am anticipating is with the increase in Establishment Reps, the authority and individual HTs will fail to grasp their significance and wonder why they will need facility time if "[I] already has time to do this". The LA will have to be strong about this' (Personal Record 4).

'...there is probably a need for us to reach out more to make sure everyone knows what we might be able to do for them. The forthcoming [CPD] event is a bit of publicity. We'll also put something in the next local association bulletin. We've had a bit in before. We did have a few requests to speak in schools and to give individual advice but I'm sure there are more people who could ask if they knew they could' (Personal Record 5).

The issues raised in the above comments to a degree overlap points made in previous chapters. However, there are common themes emerging, firstly, the need to interact with colleagues and CPD events seem to be the initial starting point for LRs to raise their profile and attract "punters through the door" and secondly, having the ability to carry out their role. Both local authorities and school management need to examine the facilities agreements (if any) they have in place and ensure that they are acting both in the letter and spirit of the legislation and accompanying ACAS code (as highlighted above). It may well be that local authorities should follow the lead of Aberdeenshire Council and put together a learning agreement that specifies the role and responsibilities of EIS LRs and also the commitment of the authority to both the lifelong learning and professional development agendas as per the Scottish Government's (2007) policy initiative and the *21ˢᵗ Century Agreement* (SEED, 2001).

Such an approach is backed up by both Alexandrou (2007) and Wallis and Stuart (2007) who highlight the positive effects learning agreements have on workplace learning.

The next part of the chapter will look to the future in terms of analysing the views of LRs as to how they believe their role should develop.

Learning Representatives' Views on their Role and its Development

A number of the respondents who completed personal records dealt with the issue of their role and future direction. The following comments encapsulate the commitment and dedication of this LR cohort; how they are not prepared to stand still and are willing to make more personal sacrifices for the benefit of their colleagues:

'How is the role progressing? It's all infrastructure stuff. Making contacts, friends and influencing people – building networks. This month, in fact next week 18 July, I have been invited to a cross council ULR meeting...My wife is impressed that I'm going to a meeting during my holidays. I definitely would not have contemplated it before I became an LR. I feel that if I keep pressing the correct buttons there should be a reward, for someone' (Personal Record 1).

'Establish better links with school colleagues and service provided.

Given location of school in rural community, source appropriate courses and other forms of CPD (eg peer support/mentoring) for colleagues.

Undertake Multi-Establishment LR training.

Establish links with Local Authority.

Continue to gain benefit of help and support from regular contact and meetings with LR Administrator, EIS National Office' (Personal Record 2).

'Develop CPD planning and recording.

Develop Staff Resources for Professional Development (Real and virtual!).

Liaise with colleagues in other establishments' (Personal Record 3).

'We are still in the process of developing our role. I was at a recent meeting where we discussed teacher research with Jim O'Brien – how learning reps can work with Edinburgh University to promote research in guiding teachers' practice. We'll be looking at research in CPD. That can only be useful in helping to develop and understand more fully our roles. If we become a good source of information on current research we could not only share this with teachers but perhaps help influence more the provision of the CPD provided by the authority.

In the future, I hope we'll gradually increase the opportunities to encourage more teachers to get the most out of CPD – and away from the 35 hours of box ticking.

Something we feel we could do soon is to use some of our Thu PM time out to have drop in sessions where any teacher could come with queries. Maybe these could be in different venues across the city, convenient for different groups' (Personal Record 5).

'In the future, I see my role developing as the need for teachers to obtain a source of completely impartial CPD advice grows. It has to be about awareness raising via publicity, about showcasing success stories and about reinforcing the concept of impartiality and non management involvement.

I also think it is very important that the role of L Rep is seen as non negotiating and as being separate from EIS Representative's role' (Personal Record 6).

'As per action plan [this LR produced a comprehensive action plan] *based on raising profile, communicating with members especially on a one to one basis, increasing understanding of LR role in all stakeholders…increased acceptance, promoting personal ownership of CPD by suggesting eg use of Standard for Full Registration as a means of getting away from CPD dominated by National, Local Authority and School (Head Teacher) initiatives'* (Personal Record 7).

Lyn McClintock adds to this debate with the following developments that have been initiated at national level to help aid the development of the LRs:

'We have been trying to build up a network of multi-establishment and school LRs in each area and to date this has met with varying degrees of success. In some areas the contact between the different types of LR has been quite good but in others I have had to continue to be involved in attending meetings to try and ensure that they will eventually do this as a matter of course. It is really important that they exchange information about developments at authority and school level. I will continue to pursue establishing a better network of LRs and have devised a communication protocol which will be included in the LR Handbook and on the LR website to try and encourage LRs at all levels to communicate better....

...It was agreed that an LR Working Group should be established to look at the future development of LRs and their role. LRs were asked to express an interest in being involved in this Working Group and 17 LRs have done so. The first meeting was held in February and discussed the remit of the Group... [and these are]...LR recommendations from the external evaluation; future training and development of LRs and the LR Website' (McClintock, 2007: 7).

If the LRs are to receive future training and they may well need it if they are going to take on such roles as being a mentor, then the EIS would be advised to help create a further qualification for its LRs akin to the Certificate in Professional Development (CPD) in Union Learning, that has been devised and delivered by the Centre for Trade Union Studies and Working Lives Research Institute (London Metropolitan University). As the Institute states, the course:

'...is for Union Learning Representatives, project workers, officers and any other trade unionists active or interested in Union Learning. ..The Certificate situates Union Learning within an industrial context and wider trade union agendas. It has been developed in consultation with trade unions to provide opportunities for participants to develop their understanding of what is happening in the world of lifelong learning and Union Learning as well as the wider context in which learning takes place. The Certificate aims to empower both unions and participants by providing a pathway into further study and trade union activity' (Working Lives Research Institute, 2007).

The Certificate consists of the following four modules: the struggle for workers' education; globalisation, change at work and the role of union learning; ways of learning and the learning agenda: organising, communicating and bargaining. The Certificate can be completed on a part-time basis over two years; it is flexible and for each module, students are required to attend for the equivalent of four days within a fourteen week period (Working Lives Research Institute, 2007).

Obviously, any future courses and qualifications designed for the LRs will be bespoke and not necessarily cover the same areas as the one cited above. However, it is imperative that all the LRs at some point in the future update their skills set and knowledge on a specifically designed course. It would seem sensible for the UWS to be involved in this process as it already designs and delivers the initial training courses for the EIS LRs.

Lyn McClintock goes on to argue that there:

'...has to be a more strategic approach to the development of the LRs and it seems to make sense to ask the LRs themselves how they see things developing. This Group feeds suggestions/recommendations to the internal CPD Ad Hoc Committee which is a sub-group of the Executive Committee' (McClintock, 2007: 7).

The final part of the chapter seeks to find out the effect of being a LR has had on this cohort from both a personal and professional perspective and whether their commitment to the role has been diminished by their experiences to date.

The Effect being a Learning Representatives has had on Respondents from a Personal and Professional Perspective

A number of the respondents who completed personal records made a number of observations as to the effect being a LR has had on them from both a personal and professional perspective. The following comments will show the effect has been positive and should prove an important recruitment tool for the next generation of EIS LRs:

'Consolidated view of importance of life-long learning and CPD in providing best practice and service to pupils.

Enhanced own CPD.

Updated IT skills eg learning on-line' (Personal Record 2).

'On a personal note the formal Post-graduate study CPD relating to LR qualification galvanised me into embarking on the Chartered Teacher pathway' (Personal Record 4).

'The effect on me professionally – it's extended what was already a period of personal growth – being on secondment. It's certainly been a nice balance – as I'm involved in CPD provision, I'm also thinking about it as a consumer at the same time – and on behalf of other consumers. It's helped me get the bigger picture of teacher training, development, et. I've just been looking at the "Journey to Excellence" materials and website with my fellow LR. Being LRs certainly led us to look at this in a broader sense, and thinking about how it could be used' (Personal Record 5).

'Being a L Rep has influenced my professional life tremendously. I value the training we receive, the support of colleagues from all over the country and the national perspective it offers on aspects of CPD' (Personal Record 6).

'L Rep meetings and training very useful for networking, plus usually very informative eg Matthew MacIver of GTCS. Also influences, to some extent, own choice of courses at central inset events. I want to do one of the Authority mentoring courses' (Personal Record 7).

The commitment, dedication and enthusiasm is infectious and Lyn McClintock sums this up succinctly when she states that:

'…I really enjoy the work and it is fantastic to see how far this Project has come since I started nearly four years ago. The LRs are as enthusiastic and hard working as ever and are a pleasure to work with. I can at last see an increase in contact from members for the LRs and at the end of the day that is what this is all about – encouraging and supporting members in undertaking quality CPD opportunities and helping them realise the benefits it brings not only to themselves but to their pupils too' (McClintock, 2007: 8).

The final chapter seeks to bring this book together by highlighting the key issues and themes that have emerged from this study and makes a number of observations that the EIS and other stakeholders may wish to consider to ensure that the LRs initiative become further embedded within the Scottish education system and is sustainable in the long term.

10

The Next Steps

Overview

Through its lifelong learning and skills agenda the Scottish Government (2007) has challenged trade unions to engage their members in learning and development that will benefit them as individuals and the nation in terms of being competitive in the global economy. The gauntlet has been thrown down and trade unions are expected to meet this challenge in part by developing a strong cadre of LRs. This study shows the EIS has risen to the challenge with its LRs initiative.

The second main cohort of EIS LRs is a committed and enthusiastic group. The LRs are dedicated to the cause of teacher professional development and have demonstrated (sometimes against considerable odds) they are willing to work hard, be innovative and resourceful in order to help colleagues. They achieve this by advising, guiding and supporting teachers, firstly by engaging or re-engaging them in CPD, secondly by showing them the available opportunities, and thirdly working constructively with strategic and operational stakeholders to create the learning society that will meet the economic, educational and societal aspirations of key stakeholders, notably the HMIE and Scottish Government.

The key strategic stakeholders involved in delivering and assessing teacher CPD and CT, namely the GTCS, National CPD Advisory Group and the HMIE have all noted the importance of the LRs in relation to the CPD agenda and that they have a vital role to play in helping key stakeholders in the education sector maintain the current momentum and success of the *21st Century Agreement*.

The dominant themes of this study are how the EIS LRs are developing and becoming embedded in the CPD structures at both national and local level; old enmities are being replaced with a relationship based on partnership and trust; a belief that teachers deserve the best professional development opportunities available and that teachers helped by the LRs have benefited in terms of their professional development.

The most significant development has been the growing relationship between ME LRs and their LA CPD QIO counterparts. In a short space of time the scepticism and suspicion of the officers has dissipated as they have got to understand the role of their LR colleagues. This has led to a greater understanding of how they can work together with the LRs in delivering effective CPD to teachers. There is a level of mutual respect and trust that has led to the LRs and QIOs working closely together on a number of initiatives. Most notably, organising and delivering joint CPD events. These events have helped to forge a closer working relationship between the two; brought the LRs to the attention of their colleagues and have encouraged teachers to take up professional development opportunities. Additionally, a number of the LRs now sit on CPD related working groups and committees where other stakeholders not only listen to and respect what they have to say and are willing to act upon their suggestions.

There is an emerging relationship between LRs and CPD Co-ordinators at school level. However, as the evaluation has highlighted, this relationship has yet to mature in the same manner as the relationship between the LRs and their counterparts at local authority level. Admittedly, it is early days as School LRs are a relatively new tier of LR and it will take them and those that follow in their footsteps time to bed in and establish themselves.

The LRs' relationship with headteachers has also improved since the publication of the first evaluation. Headteachers now seem to have a better understanding of the role and responsibilities of LRs and that they can be a valuable asset at school level. Particularly, in terms of helping school management devise and deliver an effective CPD strategy and convincing colleagues that engaging in professional development is beneficial to them, the school and their pupils. However, there is still a significant number of headteachers who, firstly, do not fully understand the role of LRs and, secondly, seem to be unaware of their legal obligations in relation to these representatives.

The UWS has to be congratulated on initiating changes to the LR training modules that have now made the courses more practice-based and ensured teachers training to be LRs are engaged in project work that gives them a greater understanding of the policy aspects of teacher CPD; will stand them in good stead when they advise, guide and support colleagues and they now have a mentor to guide them in the form of a senior ME LR. This can only help to improve the effectiveness and quality of the service the LRs provide teachers, which in turn is more likely to help teachers engage in professional development. This will be good news for the Scottish Government as teachers have a key role in delivering the world class workforce that it is striving for. A well motivated and developed teaching cadre can improve its practice (which will impact positively in the classroom) and raise the aspirations of those that matter the most – the pupils.

However, despite the progress that has been made there are a number of outstanding issues that have not been dealt with since the first study, and these are particularly affecting School-based LRs. The issues in question are adequate time-off, funded cover and integration within EIS local association structures. In relation to the first two, despite the issue being highlighted in the first evaluation and the recent UK Government consultation exercise (BERR, 2007) recommending that the ACAS Code of Practice be strengthened in relation to facility time and facilities, there has been little positive movement. A significant number of the LRs have no signed agreement in place. This means that both local authorities and school management are breaking both the letter and the spirit of the law by not complying with their statutory obligations. Worryingly, in some cases, EIS local associations have inadvertently or otherwise been complicit by their inaction in ensuring this is the case.

As for EIS local associations not taking School LRs under their wing, this goes against the Scottish Government's (2007) challenge to trade unions of ensuring that LRs are fully integrated into their structures at all levels. If the EIS LRs initiative is to be sustained in the long-term, ME and School-based LRs have to be accepted and integrated into their local association structures. If not it will hinder their ability to connect and engage with members, thus undermining both the teacher CPD and lifelong learning policy initiatives of the Scottish Government and education system, particularly as this evaluation has highlighted that non-connection with members is still a major issue for the LRs.

The LRs' continuing non-connection with the majority of the membership is a significant concern. If it continues to persist then it may well undermine the positive developments being achieved in terms of the partnership with LA CPD QIOs, school management's growing understanding of LRs and their role and the vital role that LRs play in promoting CPD to teachers. Audit Scotland, HMIE and the CTRG have all highlighted the slow take-up of CT and take-up of CPD opportunities differs dependent on a teacher's length of service. Notably, newer entrants are more likely to engage with CPD than their colleagues with longer service. The EIS and the other stakeholders must be innovative in their approach if they are to turn this situation around. Particularly, in encouraging the cynical teacher, the teacher who has no time and the wounded learner teacher that CPD and CT opportunities currently available will be beneficial to them from both a personal and professional perspective.

However, there is much that is positive; teachers who have been helped by the LRs are very positive about the LRs' advice and support they have received; an eagerness amongst the new generation of teachers for undertaking CPD and the success of the joint CPD events means the profile of the LRs has been raised significantly in the local authority areas where these events have been held.

Taking the Learning Representatives Initiative to the Next Level

The evidence presented in this book shows by encouraging teachers to engage in professional development the LRs are helping the Scottish Government in achieving its goals of promoting lifelong learning that will create a world class workforce and raise the aspirations of pupils.

There are lessons from this study that should be taken on board. With this and the above overview in mind, the following observations are designed to help make the LRs initiative sustainable in the long-term; continue to promote and strengthen the partnership approach to CPD between LRs and operational stakeholders and develop the LRs' role

Joint CPD events must continue to be organised and delivered and they should be held at least annually in each of the 32 local authorities. The concept should also be delivered at school level, maybe not on an individual basis, but definitely to clusters of schools with specific themes that meet local needs. The aim should be to create a stronger working relationship between both ME and School LRs and School CPD Co-ordinators.

If LRs are to be the role models, mentors and have a higher public profile through joint CPD events as advocated by both strategic and operational stakeholders, then the EIS must enter into discussions with the UWS to construct courses that will meet these demands and ensure there is a structured CPD Pathway for its LRs.

At national level the EIS needs to devise a communication strategy with two key aims. Firstly, how best to advertise the existence and benefits of utilising the services of the LRs amongst the wider membership to overcome the lack of awareness of this tier of lay representation and ensure the LRs long-term sustainability. Secondly, to promote the benefits of CPD and CT to its members who have either not yet realised or have refused to take advantage of the professional development opportunities available to them. Adopting this approach should help to raise the profile of the LRs and their engagement with members.

To increase the engagement of LRs with their colleagues the EIS should, firstly, adopt the TUC/STUC Climbing Frame ICT tool and advertise the fact that its LRs have this tool at their disposal to help teachers construct a coherent professional development plan. Secondly, all LRs should organise regular drop-in sessions and, thirdly, organise sessions where teachers who have been helped by LRs talk to other teachers both about the benefits of using the services of a LR and of the CPD and CT opportunities they have taken advantage of.

If the issues of time-off and funded cover are to be satisfactorily dealt with, each local authority should enter into a learning agreement with the EIS. The purpose of the agreement will be, firstly, to promote a partnership approach to learning and professional development. Secondly, to ensure that LRs at both ME and School level are afforded adequate facility time, facilities and funded cover to undertake their role and responsibilities effectively. Thirdly, for both local authorities and the EIS to meet the challenge set by the Scottish Government (2007) that employers and trade unions need to work in partnership by entering into local learning agreements.

If the LRs initiative is to be sustainable in the long-term, the EIS must ensure that through the constitutional route, the LRs are fully integrated at all levels within its structures. This will ensure they have the credibility and standing with national, area and lay officials and members. This will enable them to carry out their role and responsibilities with authority.

EIS Local Association officers and committees must engage more with School LRs. They should be a standing item on agendas; invited to speak at committee meetings and lay officers must help the LRs to improve headteachers' and School CPD Co-ordinators understanding of their role. This should lead to improved working relationships and the instigation of partnership initiatives such as learning agreements.

11

Postscript

The importance of the EIS LRs been recognised by colleagues and stakeholders at institutional, local and national level and now by the Scottish Union Learning Fund, which has recently awarded the EIS funding to further strengthen its LRs initiative. The funding will be used to developing and run a series of joint CPD events and to sign more learning agreements with local authorities akin to the one with Aberdeenshire Council. This additional support is already bearing fruit as two LRs have been seconded to the EIS on a part-time basis to help with the capacity building and sustainability of the initiative; several CPD events have taken place and another learning agreement has been signed with East Renfrewshire local authority with more in the pipeline. Additionally, the HMIE has begun to actively seek the views of the EIS LRs during its visits to local authorities and schools. All this is further evidence that the EIS LRs are becoming embedded within the Scottish education system.

The future is bright for the EIS LRs initiative and as this study has shown the LRs are helping stakeholders and colleagues alike to take on board the old Hebrew proverb that advises:

> *Do not confine your children to your own learning for they were born in another time.*

References

Aberdeenshire Council and Educational Institute of Scotland (2005) *Partnership Learning Agreement.* Edinburgh: Educational Institute of Scotland.

Advisory, Conciliation and Arbitration Service (2003) *Code of Practice on Time Off for Trade Union Duties and Activities.* London: Advisory, Conciliation and Arbitration Service.

Alcorn, M., National CPD Co-ordinator (2007) *Interview,* 26th March.

Alexandrou, A. (2006) *EIS Learning Representatives: An Evaluation of the Educational Institute of Scotland's First Cohort of Learning Representatives.* Edinburgh: Educational Institute of Scotland.

Alexandrou, A. (2007) *Partnership Out of Conflict: The Emergence of the Educational Institute of Scotland's Learning Representatives.* Glasgow: Humming Earth.

Audit Scotland (2006) A Mid-Term Report: A First Stage Review of the Cost and Implementation of the Teachers' Agreement A Teaching Profession for the 21st Century. Edinburgh: Audit Scotland.

British Educational Research Association (2004) *Revised Ethical Guidelines for Educational Research.* Southwell: British Educational Research Association.

Cairns, D., Her Majesty's Inspectorate of Education Assistant Chief Inspector (2007) *Interview,* 18th April.

Carlisle, F. (2007) E-mail correspondence with the author, 6th September.

Chartered Teacher Review Group(2008) *Report of the Chartered Teacher Review Group.* Edinburgh: Scottish Government.

Clough, B. (2008) Unions and Learning: An Historical Overview. *Journal of In-service Education,* Volume 34, Number 4, pp. 399-422.

Connelly, G. and McMahon, M. (2007) Chartered Teacher: Accrediting Professionalism for Scotland's Teachers – A View from the Inside, in the *Journal for In-Service Education,* Volume 33, Number 1, March, pp. 91-105.

Cowie, M. and Crawford, M. (2007) Principal Preparation – Still an Act of Faith? in *School Leadership and Management,* Volume 27, Number 2, pp. 129-146.

Creamer, E. G. (2008) 'Uses of Mixed Methods to Assess Epistemological Development'. A paper presented at the American Educational

Research Association Annual Conference, *Research on Schools, Neighborhoods and Communities: Towards Civic Responsibility* in New York, 24-28 March.

Department for Business Enterprise & Regulatory Reform (2007) *Workplace Representatives: A Review of their Facilities and Facility Time – Government Response to Public Consultation*. London: Department for Business Enterprise & Regulatory Reform.

Department for Trade and Industry (2007) *Workplace Representatives: A Review of their Facilities and Facility Time*. London: Department for Trade and Industry.

Donnelly, E. and Kiely, J. (2007) *Union Learning Representatives: Championing Unions or (Just) Learning?* Bournemouth: Centre for Organisational Effectiveness, University of Bournemouth.

Educational Institute of Scotland (2007) *EIS Membership Figures – 2007*. Edinburgh: Educational Institute of Scotland.

Gilmore, K., University of the West of Scotland, Co-ordinator of the EIS LRs Training Modules (2007) *Interview*, 21st March.

Her Majesty's Inspectorate of Education (2007a) *Teaching Scotland's Children: A Report on Progress in Implementing 'A Teaching Profession for the 21st Century'*. Livingston: Her Majesty's Inspectorate of Education.

Her Majesty's Inspectorate of Education (2007b) *Leadership for Learning: The Challenges of Leading in a Time of Change*. Livingston: Her Majesty's Inspectorate of Education.

Hollinrake, A., Antcliff, V. and Saundry, R. (2008) Explaining Activity and Exploring Experience – Findings from a Survey of Union Learning Representatives. *Industrial Relations Journal*, Volume 39, Number 5, pp. 392-410.

House, E.R. (1993) *Professional Evaluation: Social Impact and Political Consequences*. Newbury Park. Sage.

Hoque, K. and Bacon, N. (2008) Trade Unions, Union Learning Representatives and Employer-Provided Training in Britain. *British Journal of Industrial Relations*, Volume 46, Number 4, pp. 702-731.

Hyslop, F. (2008) *Cabinet Secretary for Education and Lifelong Learning's Response to the Report of the Chartered Teacher Review Group*. Speech Delivered to the National Chartered Teacher Conference, 7 June. Edinburgh: Scottish Government.

Ivankova, N. V., Topping, K. C. and Kawamura, Y. (2008) 'Using

Transformative Lens in Mixed Methods Studies in Education and Health Sciences. A paper presented at the American Educational Research Association Annual Conference, *Research on Schools, Neighborhoods and Communities: Towards Civic Responsibility* in New York, 24-28 March.

Kirkwood, M. and Christie, D. (2007) The Role of Teacher Research in Continuing Professional Development, in the *British Journal of Educational Studies*, Volume 54, Number 4, pp. 429-448.

Kushner, S. (2000) *Personalising Evaluation*. London: Sage.

Kushner, S. and Norris, N. (2007) *Dilemmas of Engagement: Evaluation and the New Public Management*. Oxford: Elsevier.

Lee, B. And Cassell, C. (2009) Learning Organizations, Employee Development and Learning Representative Schemes in the UK and New Zealand. *Journal of Workplace Learning*, 21 (1), 5-22.

Macdonald, A., Head Teacher of Johnstone High School (2007) *Interview*, 2nd August.

McCrone, G. (2000) *A Teaching Profession for the 21st Century*. Edinburgh: Scottish Executive Education Department.

McClintock, L., Educational Institute of Scotland Leaning Representatives Administrator (2007) *Personal Record*, 27th September.

Moore, S. and Ross, C. (2008) The Evolving Role of Union Learning Representatives. *Journal of In-service Education*, Volume 34, Number 4, pp. 423-440.

Murray, R., General Teaching Council of Scotland Professional Officer (CPD) (2007) *Interview*, 27th March.

Organisation for Economic Co-operation and Development (2007) *Improving School Leadership – OECD Background Report: Scotland*. Paris: Organisation for Economic Co-operation and Development.

Parliament (2002) *Employment Act 2002*. London: The Stationery Office.

Reeves, J., Turner, E., Morris, B. and Forde, C. (2005) Changing Their Minds: The Social Dynamics of School Leaders' Learning in the *Cambridge Journal of Education*, Volume 35, Number 2, pp. 253-273.

Reeves, J. (2007) Inventing the Chartered Teacher, in the *British Journal of Educational Studies*, Volume 55, Number 1, pp. 56-76.

Robertson, B. (2007) *Aberdeenshire Partnership Agreement – EIS Learning Representatives*, Personal Written Statement, 1st August.

Robinson, M., Walker, M., Kinder, K. And Haines, B. (2008) *Research into the Role of CPD Leadership in Schools.* York: National Foundation for Educational Research.

Scottish Executive (2003) *Life Through Learning Through Life.* Edinburgh: The Stationery Office.

Scottish Executive Education Department (2001) *A Teaching Profession for the 21ˢᵗ Century: Agreement Reached Following the McCrone Report.* Edinburgh: The Stationery Office.

Scottish Executive Education Department (2002) *The Scottish Qualification for Headship – Programme Outline.* Edinburgh: Scottish Executive Education Department.

Scottish Executive Education Department (2007) *Review of the Chartered Teacher Project.* Edinburgh: Scottish Executive Education Department.

Scottish Government (2007) *Skills for Scotland: A Lifelong Skills Strategy:* Edinburgh: Scottish Government.

Scottish Trades Union Congress (2007) *Scottish Union Learning: A Profile of Trade Union Learning in Scotland.* Glasgow: Scottish Trades Union Congress.

Stake, R.E. (2005) 'Qualitative Case Studies' in Denzin, N.K. and Lincoln, Y.S. (eds) *The Sage Handbook of Qualitative Research,* Third Edition, pp. 443-466. Thousand Oaks: Sage.

Teachers' TV (2008) *CPD – How Do They Do It In Scotland?* First Screened on Teachers' TV on 19ᵗʰ February. Manchester: Libra Television.

Trades Union Congress (2007) *The Union Learning Climbing Frame.* London Trades Union Congress.

Wallis, E. and Stuart, M. (2007) *A Collective Learning Culture: A Qualitative Study of Workplace Learning Agreements.* London: UnionLearn.

Wallis, E., Stuart, M. and Greenwood, I. (2005) 'Learners of the Workplace Unite!': An Empirical Examination of the UK Trade Union Learning Representative Initiative in *Work, Employment and Society,* Volume 19, Number 2, pp. 283-304.

Wojecki, A. (2007) 'I Am Not a Learner: Implications of Identity Construction in Workplace Learning'. A paper presented at the American Educational Research Association Annual Conference, *The World of Educational Quality* in Chicago, Illinois, 9 - 13 April.

Working Lives Research Institute (2007) *Certificate in Professional Development (CPD) in Union Learning.* London: Working Lives Research Institute.

Index